WOODWORKING PROJECTS

FOR THE GREAT OUTDOORS

42 Complete Step-by-Step Projects
for Campers, Hunters, Boaters,
Anglers, Gardeners, Bicyclists,
Walkers, and Photographers

By Don Geary

A Garden Way Publishing Book

STOREY

Storey Communications, Inc.
Schoolhouse Road
Pownal, Vermont 05261

Front cover photographs by Don Geary
Cover and text designed and produced by Carol Jessop
Illustrations and line drawings by Mary Lang unless otherwise noted
Edited by Roger Griffith

The name Garden Way Publishing is licensed to Storey Communications, Inc., by Garden Way, Inc.

Printed in the United States by Courier
First printing, August 1990

Library of Congress Cataloging-in-Publication Date

Geary, Don.
    Woodworking projects for the great outdoors : 42 complete step-by-step projects for campers, hunters, boaters, anglers, gardeners, bicyclists, walkers, and photographers / by Don Geary.
        p. cm.
    "A Garden Way Publishing book."
    Includes index.
    ISBN 0-88266-617-7 (cloth)
    ISBN 0-88266-616-9 (pbk.)
    1. Woodwork.   I. Title.
TT185.G43 1990
684'.08 — dc20   90-55047
                                                                CIP

TABLE OF CONTENTS
▼▼

INTRODUCTION

▼▼▼▼▼▼▼▼▼▼▼▼▼▼▼▼▼▼▼▼▼▼▼▼▼▼▼▼▼▼▼

Outdoorsmen are a funny breed. They can be depended on to get up at an unreasonable hour of the morning, drive for several hours in the dark, and then sit in a wet duck marsh waiting for ducks and geese to come within range of a shotgun. Sportsmen might also spend hours in the blazing sun just waiting for that big lunker to strike—"just one big one and we'll go home, I promise." Hunters and fishermen miss weddings, funerals, and even parts of the World Series while chasing all kinds of game.

While outdoorsmen may suffer more than the average person, they are the ones who see the most breathtaking sunrises and sunsets, feel the cool fresh air in the high places, and fish streams and rivers that are very much away from the madding crowd.

The outdoor scene is changing, even if we don't want to admit it. Campgrounds at state and national parks are packed with recreational vehicles, kids zoom around on all-terrain vehicles (often without helmets), and many lakes and rivers no longer contain fish that we would want to eat. Even finding a place to hunt can be a problem for many, and things will get worse before they get better.

The price of outdoor equipment is outrageous. A box of shotshells costs three times what it did a decade ago. Quality firearms, high-tech fishing rods, and clothing are all priced almost beyond the reach of most of us. To add insult to injury, federal, state, and local laws make it difficult to purchase or transport certain types of firearms, and the cost of non-resident hunting licenses really makes you think twice about hunting out of state.

It is almost easier to give up the outdoors and watch TV than it is to fish in fishless lakes, pay unheard of prices for outdoor gear, and try to find a place to hunt pheasants. But a true outdoorsman keeps going, even though the present going is a little tough. Sportsmen's organizations such as Trout Unlimited and Ducks Unlimited, the Rocky Mountain Elk Foundation, and others are working to improve the outdoors that we so enjoy. One way we can all help is to get involved and make things happen.

The purpose of *Woodworking Projects for the Great Outdoors* is to offer a number of worthwhile projects that should prove useful. Many of the projects will save you money while giving you an opportunity to make outdoor gear that is functional.

I hope, as you use this book, that you will benefit on a number of levels. I hope also that you will become a true sport and help those who are not outdoor oriented to see why we want to preserve the great outdoors not only for ourselves but for all of the generations that will follow.

No book is ever the work of one person and *Woodworking Projects for the Great Outdoors* is no exception. I would like to thank my illustrator, Mary Lang, who was unfailing in helping with many of the illustrations in the book. Information and photographs also came from the American Plywood Association, the California Redwood Association, and Porter-Cable Tools. I would also like to thank all of the sportsmen I have met over the years who have helped me to see the flowers in the forest. Lastly, I would like to thank my dad, who first introduced me to the great outdoors.

CHAPTER 1
TOOLS, MATERIALS & TECHNIQUES
▼▼▼▼▼▼▼▼▼▼▼▼▼▼▼▼▼▼▼▼▼▼▼▼▼▼▼▼▼▼▼▼▼▼▼▼▼▼▼

While a high-tech home woodworking shop is not required for any of the projects in this book, a place to plan, construct, and finish a project will make the task much more enjoyable and easy. The location will, of course, depend on how much space you have in your home. Generally speaking, a corner of the garage or basement, roughly 10' x 10', should be more than adequate for almost any do-it-yourself woodworking project.

A number of hand and power tools will make constructing woodworking projects possible. At this time, it is probably a safe assumption that the reader owns several hand and power tools. In this section we will have a look at what I consider to be some of the important and most useful tools for the do-it-yourself woodworker.

SAWS

Since most of the projects in this book use plywood, a table (bench) saw is probably the most useful of all electrical saws for the woodworker building them. The radial arm saw is similar to it, but cuts from above the work instead of below.

But you can build these projects without either one of these saws. You can make all of the plywood cuts with a hand-held circular saw with a blade size of 7¼" in diameter. A hand-held circular saw has many advantages over a stationary table saw, including a very low price tag and portability, and it is reasonably accurate. If your home workshop space is limited, as is your pocketbook, a hand-held circular saw is a good choice.

A fairly recent addition to most circular saw manufacturers' lines is the 6" (blade diameter) hand-held circular saw. This saw is ideal for cutting all types of paneling and plywood, but is not generally suitable for cutting dimensional lumber (such as 2x4s) because the cut is not deep enough.

▼▼▼▼▼▼▼▼▼▼▼▼▼▼▼▼▼▼▼▼▼▼

A 6" hand-held circular saw is a good tool for cutting plywood.

▲▲▲▲▲▲▲▲▲▲▲▲▲▲▲▲▲▲▲▲▲▲▲▲

A number of features and attachments will make this tool much more versatile. The features include adjustments for depth of cut and for angle of cut (commonly up to a 45° angle). Useful attachments include a ripping guide and vacuum hose attachment or dust bag. In addition, there are a number of after-market accessories, such as edge guides for ripping, that increase the overall usefulness of any quality hand-held circular saw.

A variety of circular saw blades is available for the do-it-yourself woodworker. It is important to use the proper circular saw blade for the cutting task at hand. A plywood blade, for example, will help you to make perfect cuts in plywood but will be of little value for cutting dimensional lumber.

▼▼▼▼▼▼▼▼▼▼▼▼▼▼▼▼▼▼▼▼▼▼

A bayonet saw is very useful for making contour cuts in plywood.

▲▲▲▲▲▲▲▲▲▲▲▲▲▲▲▲▲▲▲▲▲▲▲

Another useful saw is the saber saw or bayonet saw. According to industry sales figures, a saber saw is the most popular of all woodworking tools. It's also the first saw that many do-it-yourselfers purchase. It is useful for a variety of cutting jobs. The blade (there are many different types) is the reciprocating (up and down) type and cuts on the upstroke. A saber saw is invaluable for making curved cuts. Special purpose blades of various lengths are available. As a rule, use the finest tooth blade possible to get a smooth, even cut. The better saber saws have a tilting base, so bevel cuts can be easily made, and a variable speed motor.

MISCELLANEOUS POWER TOOLS

A number of useful power tools are available to the do-it-yourself woodworker. We will look at these in this section. All of these specialty tools make woodworking easier and more enjoyable for the average woodworker. More important, they will enable the nonprofessional to achieve truly professional results.

SANDERS

While sanding of any woodworking project can be done with a sanding block and plenty of elbow grease, an electrically powered sanding tool will make the work go much faster and with less effort. Two types of hand sanders, belt sanders and orbital sanders, are in use today, and both have many uses around the home woodworking shop.

Belt sanders turn a belt of sandpaper around two drums for rapid material removal. Use two hands when operating this tool. It works best when kept moving while you sand parallel to the grain of the wood. The weight of the machine is more than ample for effective sanding, but by pressing down while moving with the grain, it is possible to remove material faster.

A belt sander can be used for shaping or adding contour to a project, but this must be done carefully because of the tool's ability to remove material quickly.

Sanding belts are available in fine, medium, and coarse grits.

Orbital sanders, which are often called finish sanders, are used primarily for the final sanding of a project prior to applying a surface finish. While orbital sanders can be used to remove high spots and round edges, their primary function is to prepare a surface for finishing, and they do this very well. A finish sander will save hours of final sanding and do a much better job than a simple sanding block.

A wide range of sand papers, from 80 grit to 400 grit, is available for most orbital sanders. Some orbital sanders require die cut paper while others can use any type of sandpaper, providing it is cut to fit the unit.

ROUTER

A hand-held router was at one time only found in a professional woodworking shop. Now it has become quite popular with do-it-yourself woodworkers. At least part of the popularity of a hand-held router lies in its ability to perform a number of tasks better and more quickly than other tools. While a major use for this tool is adding a decorative edge to material, kitchen cabinet doors and counter edges, for example, a router can also be used for making dados and rabbet joints and, with special attachments, dovetail joints.

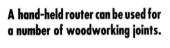

A hand-held router can be used for a number of woodworking joints.

A rating of around 1½ horsepower is more than adequate for the do-it-yourself woodworker's router. A router in this class will have a speed of around 22,000 rpm, which is suitable for all do-it-yourself and most professional woodworking. Other features that are handy include a work light (installed just below the motor of the unit), a transparent plastic shield which protects the user from flying wood chips, a zero reset feature, a shaft lock which makes changing bits easier, and a dust collection system. As might be expected, these features add to the price of a router but are worthwhile additions for more than casual woodworkers.

Router bits are the business end of the router. There is a wide selection to choose from. Most companies offer router bit sets, which contain up to forty router bits. These can be quite expensive and often contain router bits that are rarely used. As a rule it is probably best to purchase specific router bits for a project. Router bits are all made from high speed steel. In addition, many router bits are carbide-tipped, which not only dramatically extends their life but makes a cleaner, smoother cut. Carbide-tipped router bits commonly cost twice as much as high speed steel router bits but stay sharp through extended use.

All router bits tend to turn black with use. This discoloration is usually a surface film composed of wood sap heated by friction. Router bits work most effectively when clean. Unplug the router, then rub the bit with a rag dipped in turpentine. Stubborn residue can usually be removed by wire brushing. Many woodworkers spray a light coating of silicone lubricant on a router blade (or any tool blade) before use. Too much lubricant can stain the wood being worked. A light coating is all that is needed to prevent resin build up on the bit.

ELECTRIC DRILLS

Electric drills are popular in America today, and almost every household has at least one model. A number of attachments are available that can quickly turn a standard drill into a polisher, sander, and even a powerful screwdriver. Some of the more worthwhile features of an electric drill include a variable speed motor, reversing capability, and a long power cord.

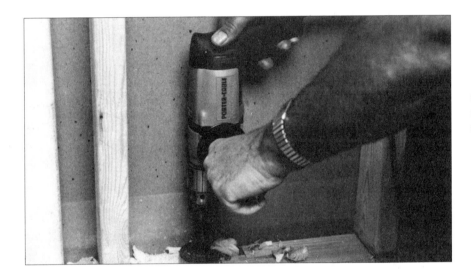

▼▼▼▼▼▼▼▼▼▼▼▼▼▼▼▼▼▼▼▼▼

An electric drill has many uses around the home and woodworking shop.

▲▲▲▲▲▲▲▲▲▲▲▲▲▲▲▲▲▲▲▲▲

Power screw drills, or "screw guns," as they are called in the trade, are used by professional dry wall hangers for hanging Sheetrock. These tools are also useful for screwing down decking and in other projects where strength comes from screws rather than from nailing. Cordless models are handy for small projects, and electrically powered models are ideal for production work.

Increasing in popularity are cordless drills. The better made models work almost as well as electrically powered units with the distinct advantage of not requiring cords and a source of commercial electrical power, relying instead on one or more rechargeable battery packs.

A variety of drill bits is available to the woodworker. In addition to the standard high-speed twist drill bits (the most common type), there are special-purpose drill bits designed for woodworking. These include spade bits, countersink bits, hole cutters, and Forstner bits.

A number of the projects contained in this book, whirligigs, for example, require precise drilling of several parts. While this drilling can be accomplished by careful hand alignment, a drill press will make the work go much smoother and often give better results. Drill stands, into which a standard electric drill can be attached, are inexpensive and easy to use. Free-standing or bench-mounted drill presses bore wood and metal precisely but are generally not part of the do-it-yourselfer's workshop.

MATERIALS

PLYWOOD

Since most of the projects in this book are constructed with plywood, it may be helpful to discuss this modern building material in some detail. The accompanying table explains the different grades of plywood as defined by the American Plywood Association.

Plywood is a flat panel which is built up of an odd number of sheets of wood, or veneers, and assembled under pressure using adhesives to create a finished panel. Plywood is probably the most common building material in use today. It does not warp, and is much stronger and less expensive than solid lumber.

There are two broad categories of plywood, exterior and interior grade.

Exterior plywood is made with waterproof glue. It can be exposed to the weather for an indefinite period of time and the layers or plies will not separate. The chart shows the many grades within the exterior classification.

Interior plywood is made with a highly moisture-resistant but not waterproof glue. It is possible to special order interior grade plywood which has been constructed with a waterproof glue. This is commonly used for constructing kitchen cabinets or bathroom vanities where appearance as well as being waterproof are requirements.

Interior grades are generally considered to be appearance grades. They are commonly used inside the home, for cabinets, paneling, and furniture, where they are quite visible. A number of exterior grades also have an appearance grade designation—exterior siding, for example.

REDWOOD

Redwood is one of the most beautiful and useful of our native American softwoods. It is easily worked with hand or power tools and is naturally resistant to decay, so can be placed in direct contact with soil or water, such as in building decks or docks. Unfortunately, our supply of redwood is finite and, while not a rare wood, it is expensive when compared with more common building materials. The price of redwood at your local lumber yard or home improvement center is related to how far you are from northern

Plywood Grades for Exterior Uses

GRADE (EXTERIOR)	FACE	BACK	INNER PLIES	USES
A-A	A	A	C	Outdoor, where appearance of both sides is important.
A-B	A	B	C	Alternate for A-A, where appearance of one side is less important. Face is finish grade.
A-C	A	C	C	Soffits, fences, base for coatings.
B-C	B	C	C	For utility uses such as farm buildings, some kinds of fences, etc., base for coatings.
303© Siding	C (or better)	C	C	Panels with variety of surface texture and grooving patterns. For siding, fences, paneling, screens, etc.
T 1-11©	C	C	C	Special ⅝" panel with deep parallel grooves. Available unsanded, textured, or MDO surface.
C-C (plugged)	C (plugged)	C	C	Excellent base for tile and linoleum, backing for wall coverings, high-performance coatings.
C-C	C	C	C	Unsanded, for backing and rough construction exposed to weather.
B-B Plyform	B	B	C	Concrete forms. Re-use until wood literally wears out.
MDO	B	B or C	C	Medium Density Overlay. Ideal base for paint; for siding, built-ins, signs, displays.
HDO	A or B	A or B	C-Plugged or C	High Density Overlay. Hard surface; no paint needed. For concrete forms, cabinets, counter tops, tanks.

Plywood Grades for Interior Uses

GRADE (EXTERIOR)	FACE	BACK	INNER PLIES	USES
A-A	A	A	D	Cabinet doors, built-ins, furniture where both sides will show.
A-B	A	B	D	Alternate of A-A. Face is finish grade, back is solid and smooth.
A-D	A	D	D	Finish grade face for paneling, built-ins, backing.
B-D	B	D	D	Utility grade. For backing, cabinet sides, etc.
C-D	C	D	D	Sheathing and Structural uses such as temporary enclosures, subfloor. Unsanded.
Underlayment	C-Plugged	D	C and D	For underlayment or combination subfloor-underlayment under

The capital letters in the three columns describing the piles refer to the quality of the wood used. A, the best, is smooth and paintable. B will have circular repair plugs and tight knots. C has knotholes and splits. D has similar but larger flaws.

California and some parts of the Pacific Northwest.

To give you an example, a friend in Virginia recently built a 12' x 40' redwood deck at a cost of around $1,500. Another friend, around Sacramento, California, built a similar deck for around $600. The dramatic difference in material costs is directly related to the fact that the redwood purchased in Virginia had to be trucked more than 2,000 miles but the redwood used for the California deck was grown near the site.

Redwood is an excellent choice for outdoor building projects providing the cost is not prohibitive. Redwood has no toxicity and your finished projects will look beautiful. Heart redwood has a natural resistance to weather and diseases that attack other woods. Some grades that you will find in lumber yards are not all heartwood but have some cream-colored sapwood. Sapwood is not decay-resistant and should be used only above the ground.

The accompanying chart explains the various grades and uses.

Redwood Grades and Uses

	CLEAR ALL HEART	CLEAR	B GRADE	CONSTRUCTION HEART	CONSTRUCTION COMMON	MERCHANTABLE HEART	MERCHANTABLE
ARCHETECTURAL	■	■	■	-----	-----	-----	-----
GARDEN	-----	-----	-----	■	■	■	■
KNOTS	-----	-----	■	■	■	■	■
SAPWOODS	-----	■	■	-----	■	-----	■
POSTS	■	-----	-----	■□	-----	-----	-----
BEAMS	■	-----	-----	■□	-----	-----	-----
JOISTS	■	-----	-----	■□	-----	-----	-----
DECKING	■	■	■	■	■□	-----	-----
RAILS	■	■	■	■	■□	-----	-----
FENCEBOARDS	■	■	■	■	■	■	■□
BENCHES	■	■	■	■	■	■	■□
PLANTERS	■	-----	-----	■	-----	■□	-----
TRELLISES	■	■	■	■	■	■	■□
FURNITURE	■	■	■	■	■	■	■□

■ SUITABLE GRADE FOR USE
□ MOST ECONOMICAL GRADE FOR USE

TREATED LUMBER

In many parts of the United States, especially where redwood is expensive, the only alternative for outdoor building projects is to use some type of treated lumber. There are several types. Untreated lumber in contact with soil or exposed weather will last three to five years. Pressure-treated lumber will last many more years when used either above or below the ground.

Wood treated with chromated copper arsenate (CCA-treated) generally needs no additional protective coating, even for "frequent human contact" uses such as decks, planting boxes, and picnic tables. CCA-treated lumber is safe to use outdoors when sawdust and construction debris are cleaned up and disposed of after construction.

Lumber has been pressure-treated since Biblical times. Some of the methods result in a potentially toxic product, and these should be avoided. A good example of a toxic substance is the creosote used in preserving railroad ties. Use of wood products that have a toxic residue may have short- or long-term ill effects around your home and garden. If you are considering purchasing treated lumber, buy only lumber that has a label telling you that it was treated according to approved guidelines.

Two basic types of preservatives are used today, one is oil-based, the other waterborne. The wood is submerged and pressure forces the chemicals into the pores of the wood. The green color seen in some treated woods is the result of waterborne salts, such as inorganic arsenicals. Oil-based preservatives generally give wood a dark brown, almost black, color.

When working with treated lumber, observe basic safety rules. Wear eye protection, a dust mask, and gloves. Avoid inhaling sawdust when cutting treated lumber. Wash thoroughly with soap and water after handling it. Seal the wood when you use it for high traffic areas, such as benches and decks.

WOODWORKING JOINTS

A number of woodworking joints are used for building projects in this book. By following the instructions, you should have no trouble constructing them.

BUTT JOINT

The simplest of all woodworking joints, the butt joint is made by attaching one edge of a material to another with glue and nails or screws. While this is certainly not the strongest of all wood joints, it is a good choice for projects such as drawer bottoms and simple boxes. This joint is very easy to make, it is reasonably strong, and if the joining pieces are cut true, it is almost foolproof. A butt joint can be used on the end of a project or in the middle, for shelving or internal dividers in a camp kitchen, for example.

Square, smooth edges on the mating surfaces of the pieces are essential.

A table saw or hand-held circular saw, used with a cutting guide for the saw, will help you to achieve square and true edges on pieces of plywood that are used for the butt joint. A few drops of adhesive along the mating surfaces will add strength to this joint. Most butt joints are also nailed or screwed to keep the pieces aligned as the adhesive sets and to add strength to the joint.

▼▼▼▼▼▼▼▼▼▼▼▼▼▼▼▼▼▼▼▼▼▼▼

Two types of butt joints.

▲▲▲▲▲▲▲▲▲▲▲▲▲▲▲▲▲▲▲▲▲▲▲

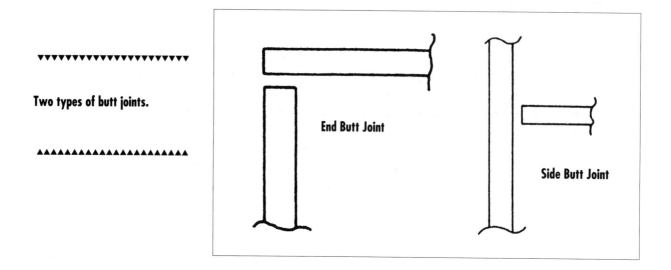

End Butt Joint

Side Butt Joint

The heads of these fasteners should be concealed if visible on the surface. This can be done by countersinking the nail or screw head, then filling the depression with a paste-type filler material. An alternative to this is to use filler plugs of wooden dowel. Give these plugs a light coat of glue, insert them in the hole over the fastener heads, then, after the glue has set, sand them flush with the surface.

▼▼▼▼▼▼▼▼▼▼▼▼▼▼▼▼▼▼▼▼▼▼▼

Wood filler plugs are used to fill nail or screw holes.

▲▲▲▲▲▲▲▲▲▲▲▲▲▲▲▲▲▲▲▲▲▲▲

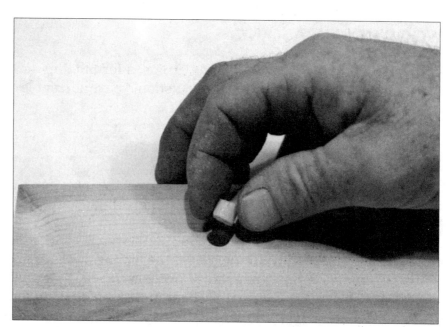

RABBET JOINT

The rabbet joint is easy to make and is stronger than the simple butt joint. It is a good choice for drawer bottoms, cabinet sides, or wherever you want a concealed joint. It is constructed by removing a section of wood that is equal to the thickness of the joining piece of lumber. Rabbet joints made with plywood will conceal the end grain of the joining piece of plywood.

A successful rabbet joint, or any woodworking joint, for that matter, must have square-ended pieces. Because a section of one of the mating surfaces must be removed, more than casual accuracy in cutting is required. The best rabbet joints are made on a table saw or radial arm saw but, with careful set-up and cutting, can also be made with a hand-held circular saw. One good alternative is to use a hand-held router with a straight bit. Setting up for the routing, measuring and marking carefully, and an edge guide for the router during the cutting will ensure a good rabbet joint.

Rabbet joints are always glued and often also nailed or screwed. If glue alone is used, the joint must be clamped until the glue sets completely. If nails or screws are used, they should be driven through an edge that will be concealed or, if exposed, countersunk and the holes filled, then sanded flush with the face of the project.

Three types of rabbet joints are used in projects in this book. The first is the *edge rabbet joint*, which is a good choice when one edge of a plywood panel is to be concealed. This is a very strong joint. To construct it, the mating edges of the wood are cut along the entire mating surface to a depth of approximately one-half of their thickness. Both edges are rabbet cut before the project is assembled. Then, when the pieces are assembled, one of the edges will be concealed. This long joint requires careful measuring, marking, and cutting. A table saw or hand-held router are the best tools for making this joint.

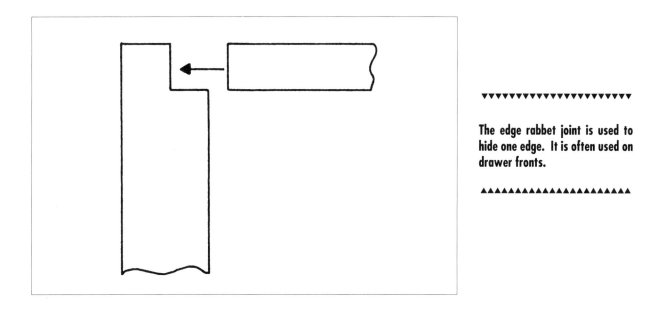

▼▼▼▼▼▼▼▼▼▼▼▼▼▼▼▼▼▼▼▼▼▼▼

The edge rabbet joint is used to hide one edge. It is often used on drawer fronts.

▲▲▲▲▲▲▲▲▲▲▲▲▲▲▲▲▲▲▲▲▲▲▲

The second useful rabbet joint is the *double rabbet joint*, and it is similar to the edge joint. It is a very strong woodworking joint that offers concealment of one entire edge of the two mating surfaces.

▼▼▼▼▼▼▼▼▼▼▼▼▼▼▼▼▼▼▼▼▼▼

The double rabbet joint is very strong.

▲▲▲▲▲▲▲▲▲▲▲▲▲▲▲▲▲▲▲▲▲▲▲▲▲

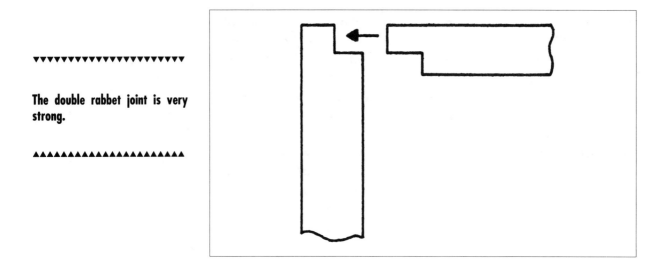

The third joint is called the *back panel rabbet joint*, and it can be used for installing a back panel on a plywood project such as a camp kitchen. To make this joint, a rabbet cut is made all the way around the interior edges of a project—a box for example.

Great care must be exercised in making this cut, and the panel itself must be cut precisely. Make the rabbet cuts on all edges before assembling

▼▼▼▼▼▼▼▼▼▼▼▼▼▼▼▼▼▼▼▼▼▼

The back panel rabbet joint is used to mount rear panel firmly.

▲▲▲▲▲▲▲▲▲▲▲▲▲▲▲▲▲▲▲▲▲▲▲▲▲

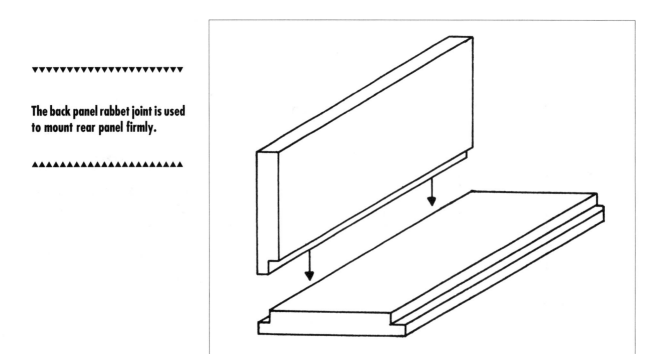

the project rather than trying to make the cut just prior to inserting the back panel. The back panel rabbet joint offers great strength and a bit of a challenge for the do-it-yourself woodworker.

DADO JOINT

Dado joints are similar to rabbet joints in that a cut is made to receive another piece, except that they are not made on the edge of a project. Dado joints are commonly used for shelving and dividers where these pieces are in a permanent position. The simple dado joint consists of a groove that is cut out of the vertical members of the unit and a shelf that is cut squarely. Dado joints add great strength to any project.

Many woodworkers use a table saw fitted with a special dado blade for making dado cuts. I have found a hand-held router fitted with a carbide-

▼▼▼▼▼▼▼▼▼▼▼▼▼▼▼▼▼▼▼▼▼▼▼▼

The basic dado joint, used to join the end or edge of one board into the cut surface of another.

▲▲▲▲▲▲▲▲▲▲▲▲▲▲▲▲▲▲▲▲▲▲▲▲

tipped, straight bit to be the best tool. This is especially true when working with large sheets of plywood because it is much easier to work on top of the sheet with a router than to try to maneuver the sheet on a table saw. One other point in favor of a router over a table saw is that a straight bit for a router costs only a few dollars (even for a carbide-tipped bit) while a quality dado saw blade set for a table saw will cost more than $50.

Two other versions of the dado joint are worth mentioning. These are the *dado/rabbet joint* and the *stop dado joint*. While both of these joints require extra care and work, they offer greater strength and a professional-looking flair as well.

The dado/rabbet joint is a combination of the dado and rabbet wood-working joints. An example of this joint might best illustrate how it is constructed. Suppose you are building a field box for cameras and optical equipment which will have internal dividers. After you have determined the spacing for the dividers you will make dado cuts on the side pieces of the box,

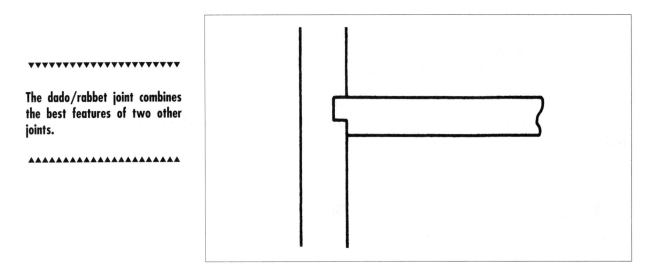

but only to a thickness of one-half the thickness of the dividers. Then you will make a rabbet cut on both ends of the dividers equal to the thickness of the dado cuts made previously. The dividers are then inserted into the sidewalls of the box and you have a strong dado/rabbet joint.

The stop dado woodworking joint also requires working on both pieces of the project, the internal divider and the sidewalls in the previous example, but the end result is a concealed edge joint for the divider. To make this joint,

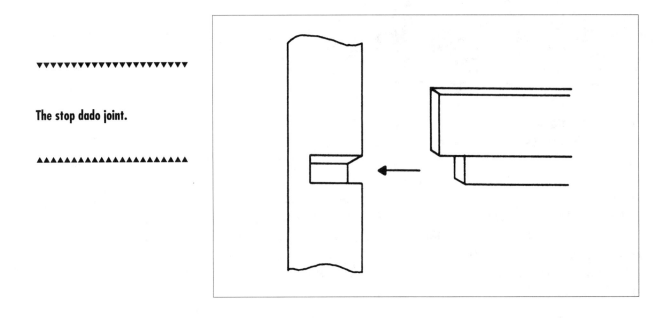

cut a dado from the back edge of the sidewall and stop at least 1" from the forward edge. It will be necessary to do a little chisel work to the inside of the dado cut to make it square when using a dado blade, but is not required when a router is used. Next, the divider is cut to fit exactly inside the dado. The divider is inserted into the dado cut. From the side of the project, the joint between the sidewall and the divider will not be visible.

LAP JOINT

Lap joints are not often used when building projects with plywood, but there are a few cases where this joint can be handy. A lap joint is made by removing equal parts of plywood from the mating surfaces of both pieces. When the two pieces are then fitted together, the resulting thickness will be equal to one of the pieces. Success in making a lap joint depends a great deal on planning, accurate layout, and precise cutting. It is important that the mating pieces fit together snugly for appearance and strength. Stationary power tools such as a table saw or radial arm saw will help you make accurate cuts in plywood. A hand-held router, fitted with a straight bit and used with some type of guidance system, can also be used for making lap joints.

One useful lap joint when working with plywood is called the *edge cross-lap joint*. With this lap joint, equal parts are removed from the two pieces to be joined. Then the pieces are fitted together for a very strong and attractive joint.

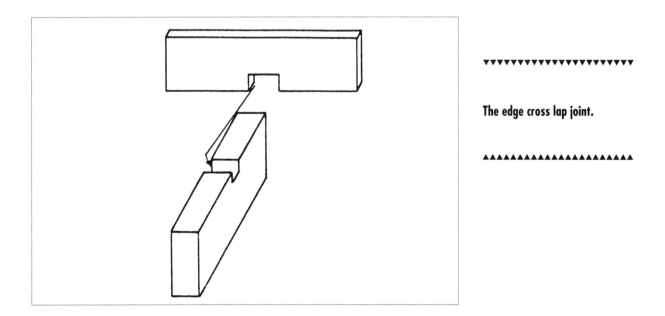

▼▼▼▼▼▼▼▼▼▼▼▼▼▼▼▼▼▼▼▼▼▼▼▼

The edge cross lap joint.

▲▲▲▲▲▲▲▲▲▲▲▲▲▲▲▲▲▲▲▲▲▲▲▲

DOVETAIL JOINT

Dovetail joints require the most work to complete and are therefore best used on projects where you want to add a little personal flair, the drawers on a fly tier's cabinet for example. While it is possible to plan and cut a dovetail joint with a handsaw designed for the purpose, a better method involves the use of a router and a dovetail template.

Dovetailing with a router is an exercise in setting up the work pieces and a special template. Next, a router is used to carve out the dovetail detail with the aid of the template to guide the router.

Dovetail joints are always glued and rarely nailed or screwed. Clamp the pieces together while the adhesive sets.

ADHESIVES

A number of different types of adhesive are useful for the do-it-yourselfer. The most useful adhesives for building outdoor projects are the waterproof type.

Resorcinol glue is an excellent choice if the project will come in contact with moisture or water. This is an extremely strong resin-type adhesive. Less than perfect woodworking joints can be made stronger because of the good gap-filling capability of this adhesive. It must be used at temperatures of at least 70 degrees Fahrenheit both during application and setup, which takes about sixteen hours. Resorcinol glue is only available in powdered form and it must be mixed just prior to use. Pot life—the amount of time the glue mixture will remain workable and usable—is approximately four hours. In use, mating surfaces are given a light coat of the adhesive, fitted together, then clamped until the adhesive sets.

Polyvinyl Resin, commonly known as white glue, is one of the most popular adhesives around the home and workshop. It is a good general-purpose adhesive that can be applied over a wide range of temperatures and usually sets in about two hours. It is a poor choice, however, if the project will be exposed to moisture or if great strength is required.

Aliphatic resin is one of the strongest and best choices of a woodworking adhesive providing the project will not be exposed to high moisture levels. Aliphatic resin is excellent for less than perfect woodworking joints because it has good gap-filling capabilities. It is easy to work with because it does not set up very fast and it can be used at temperatures as low as 45 degrees Fahrenheit. Aliphatic resin is nonstaining. Once hardened, excess glue can be sanded off.

Plastic resin is a good choice if the woodworking project requires a water-resistant adhesive. It is more difficult to work with than aliphatic resin, but it has some very desirable characteristics. It is a good general-purpose adhesive for use in the woodworking shop providing the project has tight-fitting joints. It is slightly difficult to work with because it requires a temperature of at least 70 degrees Fahrenheit. The glued project must remain clamped and undisturbed for sixteen hours for best results.

Casin glue is a strong, general-purpose adhesive which is made from milk. It is reasonably water-resistant, with good gap-filling capabilities and can be used at any temperatures above freezing. Casin glue is available in powdered form and must be mixed just prior to use. Setting time is around four hours, and the project should be clamped during this time.

Hot melt glues. There are several types and all are a good choice for assembling small pieces of a project quickly. As soon as hot melt glue is applied it begins to cool and harden. It is good for filling gaps but is not as strong as other types of adhesives.

Contact cement is a good choice when the mating surfaces are large, such as attaching a layer of veneer to a plywood surface. Contact cement is available in water-base or solvent-base formulations. As a rule, water-base contact cement is a better choice for the do-it-yourself woodworker because solvent-base contact cement is highly flammable and potentially toxic. Check the container label before purchase.

Construction adhesives. Those applied with a caulking gun have a number of uses for the outdoor woodworker. Several types are available and some might be just right for your project needs. Foam board adhesive is a good choice when layering foam panels for making duck decoy bodies. Panel adhesive, deck adhesive, and sub-floor adhesive are good choices where a strong, waterproof glue is required.

FINISHES

Once your have constructed an outdoor project you will be wise to give it a coating or two of some type of finish to seal the wood (helping to waterproof it) make the project look nicer. Some projects, such as goose and duck decoys, are not finished until they have been painted to resemble live geese and ducks.

For our purposes, finish materials include fillers, sealers, primers, paints, clear finishes, stains, and oils.

Fillers are used as the first step in the finishing process to fill the pores of wood, and particularly those with large pores, such as oak, ash, and walnut. Fillers may also be used to add color or tone prior to applying a clear finish coating. Fillers are not required for softwoods such as fir, pine, or poplar but an application of a sealer is generally recommended.

Sealers are necessary for a surface that has been filled to prevent the filler from migrating into the finish coating. Sealers are also a good idea for closed grain woods, especially plywood. There are two types of sealers, shellac and synthetic resin. Shellac sealer is made by mixing one part four-pound-cut shellac (white) to seven parts alcohol. The shellac sealer is brushed on and allowed to dry before the finish coats are applied. Synthetic resin sealers are sold ready for use and are recommended for plywood projects. Synthetic sealers are applied with a brush and help to prevent the wood from absorbing moisture. They are used prior to applying a clear finish.

Primer is used to seal bare wood that will be painted. A primer prevents the bleeding through of knots and nails and provides a solid base for the finish coatings. All previously unpainted wood which will be finished with an oil or water base paint should first be primed. While both oil and water base primers are available, I have found that the oil base primer (in an exterior grade) seems to perform better for outdoor projects than a water-based primer.

Paint choices are vast for an outdoor project. Choose a quality paint, price is usually a fair guide for quality here, in a color that is suitable for the project. Latex paints are about as durable as oil base paints and, because tools (and the painter) can be cleaned with water, are probably a better choice for the nonprofessional woodworker.

Stains give a project a natural wood grain look and, in some cases seal the wood as well. *Water base stains* are probably the easiest of all stains to work with. Generally sold in powder form, they must be mixed with hot water prior to use. They have a tendency to raise wood grain during application, and the project may require a light sanding before a clear finish coating is applied.

Oil stains are sold as pigment or penetrating types. *Pigment oil stains* are best for wood surfaces with an uneven color as the stain will tend to even out the overall look. Pigment oil stains do not penetrate very deeply into the surface of the wood and can be sanded off if desired. *Penetrating oil stains* are easier to apply and, as the name suggests, penetrate deeply into the surface. Both types of oil stains are available is a wide range of tones.

Sealer stains are another popular type of stain as they perform two functions, sealing and staining in one application, and therefore can save finishing time. Sealer stains are available in a wide range of wood tone colors.

Clear finishes are applied when the grain of the wood is to be shown. They include polyurethane, varnish, shellac, and linseed oil. Practically speaking, the only good choices for projects that will remain outdoors are polyurethane and boiled linseed oil.

Polyurethane is a good clear coating choice because it is resistant to stains, abrasions, acids, strong cleaners, fuels, alcohol, and many chemicals. It is easy to apply with a brush, roller, or spray and, once dry, is tough. This finish has a tendency to develop a yellowish cast over time, however, and some woodworkers find this objectionable.

Boiled linseed oil is a good finish choice for application to redwood decks and furniture. I have found that a mixture of two parts boiled linseed oil to one part paint thinner is easier to apply and penetrates better than straight linseed oil. Linseed oil brings out the natural beauty of redwood and will help to prevent cracking and checking over time. Apply linseed oil to a redwood deck every two to four years depending on the relative humidity for your area.

CHAPTER 2
CAMPING PROJECTS
▼▼▼▼▼▼▼▼▼▼▼▼▼▼▼▼▼▼▼▼▼▼▼▼

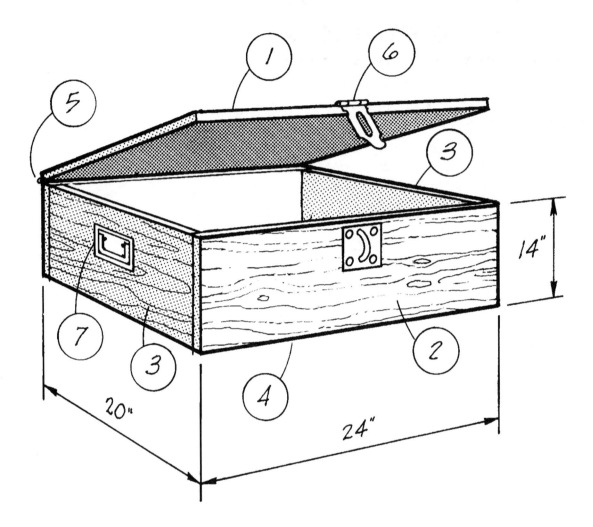

A large, covered plywood box is very handy for holding food that does not require refrigeration on a camping trip. Such a box is too large for backpackers but, for those who "car camp," canoe, or spend time in the outdoors where size is not a problem, the animal-proof food box will be greatly appreciated. This box is intended to protect foodstuffs from small mammals such as raccoons, skunks, and mice, but it will not stop a determined bear. Bears can peel open any plywood box, ice chest, or even an automobile trunk to get to the goodies therein.

The box is simple to construct and will last for decades with little care. The least expensive and durable construction material is ½" CDX plywood although a better grade plywood such as ACX or ABX offers a more attractive finish surface. The ¾" hinged cover is best when constructed from ACX plywood because the cover makes a very convenient work surface around camp.

Materials List

One-quarter sheet ¾" ABX plywood and one-half sheet ½" CDX cut as follows:

1. Top: ¾" ABX plywood, 20" x 24"
2. Front and back: ½" CDX plywood, 14" x 24" (two required)
3. Sides: ½" CDX plywood, 14" x 19" (two required)
4. Bottom: ½" CDX plywood, 19" x 23"
5. Piano hinge: 24"
6. Hasp
7. Concealed handles (two required)
   One quart each, exterior primer and paint
   One tube caulking and one tube waterproof construction
     adhesive
   6d finishing nails

Cut all pieces according to the materials list. Nail the front, back, and sides to the bottom. Use waterproof construction adhesive and tack with 6d finishing nails (galvanized) to hold the pieces together while the adhesive sets.

Before attaching the top, caulk all interior seams with a good grade, silicone-based exterior caulking which is labeled "paintable." This will help to keep the box waterproof.

Attach the piano hinge to the cover with screws, then attach the cover and hinge to the back of the box. Coat all surfaces of the box with an exterior grade primer. When this dries, apply one or more coats of exterior grade finish coating. I like to paint the interior of the box white and all exterior surfaces forest green.

After the paint has dried, attach the galvanized concealed handles to both sides, about 6" down from the top and centered. Next, attach the latch to the top and front of the box.

This box is large enough to hold food and kitchen gear for a week-long trip for about four people, and it can be carried by one person. You can enlarge or reduce the size of the box to fit your specific needs.

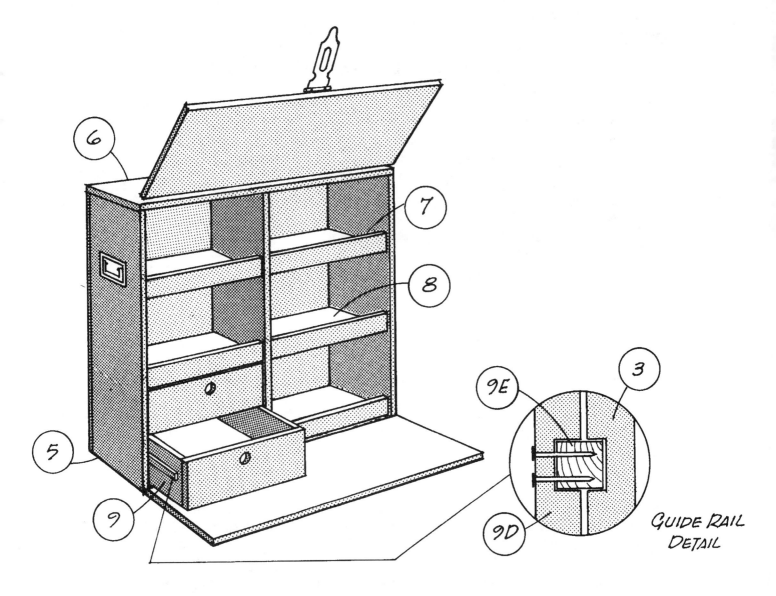

GUIDE RAIL
DETAIL

If you do a lot of car camping, either at established campgrounds or in national forests, you will find the camp kitchen a very handy piece of equipment because almost all of your kitchen needs can easily be contained in a sturdy, movable unit.

The unit shown is designed to be placed on one end of a picnic table or truck tailgate, and is not free-standing. If you want it to be free-standing, you must fashion a bracket for both sides. Into these brackets will slip four legs to hold up the unit.

One version of the camp kitchen I designed was free-standing but the rigors of camp life and the elements of wind and rain proved too much for the unit. Therefore I do not recommend it.

Materials List

▼▼▼▼▼▼▼▼▼▼▼▼▼▼▼▼▼▼▼▼▼▼▼▼

One sheet ½" CDX plywood, one-quarter sheet ½" ABX plywood, one-quarter sheet ¼" Masonite, and one piece of pine, ½" x 5" x 15' cut as follows:

1. Top door: ½" plywood—14½" x 32"
2. Bottom door: ½" ABX plywood, 15" x 32"
3. Sides and divider: ½" plywood, 9½" x 29½" (three required)
4. Back: ½" plywood, 29½" x 32"
5. Bottom: ½" plywood, 10" x 32"
6. Top: ½" plywood, 10" x 32"
7. Shelf faces: ½" pine—2" x 15¼" (five required)
8. Shelves: ½" plywood, 9" x 15¼" (four required)
   Shelf supports, ½" x ½" x 9" pine (eight required)
9. Drawers (two required)
   A. Front: ½" pine, 4⅞" x 15⅛" (two required)
   B. Back: ½" pine, 4⅞" x 15⅛" (two required)
   C. Bottom: ¼" Masonite, 9" x 10" (two required)
   D. Sides: ½" pine, 4⅞" x 8½" (four required)
   E. Guide rails: ½" x ½" x 8½" pine (four required)
10. Hinges: 3" butt hinges (two required)
11. Hasp
12. Concealed handles (two required)
13. Piano hinge, 32"
    One quart each, exterior primer and paint
    One tube each, caulking and waterproof construction adhesive
    4d and 6d finishing nails as required

▼▼▼

When building the camp kitchen, cut all pieces squarely. This will reduce problems during assembly. While a table saw or radial arm saw are two good power tool choices for cutting the plywood required for this project, the cuts can be made with a hand-held circular saw providing some type of guidance system is used to help you to make straight and true cuts.

Cut the parts as indicated in the materials list. Mark the location of the drawer guide rail channels on the left side piece and the center divider. Make

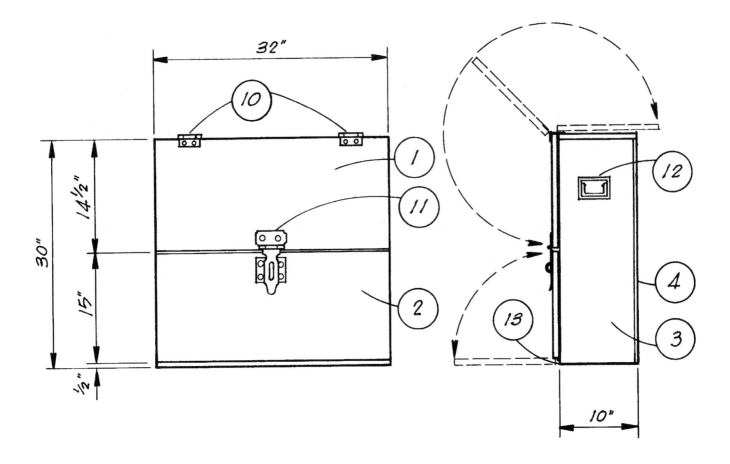

dado channels at these locations—2½" and 7½" up from the bottom. The drawer sides should be dado cut at this time, 2⅜" up from the bottom of each. All dado cuts are ½" wide and ¼" deep.

Mark the location of the brackets for the internal shelves on both sides and center divider, 10" and 20" up from the bottom. Attach the shelf support brackets (½" x ½" x 9") at these locations. Use construction adhesive and 4d finishing nails.

Assemble the two sides, top, and bottom. Use construction adhesive applied with a caulking gun, and nail with 6d finishing nails to hold the pieces together while the adhesive sets. Attach the back of the unit. In this design, the back piece is attached flush with the edges of the camp kitchen.

Insert the center divider. Use construction adhesive applied with a caulking gun, and secure with finishing nails. As an aid to proper positioning, put the shelves in place on each side of the divider, on the shelf brackets. Use adhesive and fasten the center divider with 4d finishing nails, through the top, bottom, and back of the camp kitchen.

Assemble the shelves by gluing and nailing the face boards to the shelves. Note that the faces are flush with the bottom of each shelf. Apply a bead of adhesive to the top side of each shelf bracket, then place the shelves in position. Carefully nail in place with 4d finishing nails. Nail the shelves through the back and sides of the unit and through the top of each shelf into the center divider.

Construct the drawers according to the materials list. Note that the drawer faces have a ¾" hole which is used as a finger pull for opening. The individual drawer guide rail system (see guide rail detail in illustration) is simply blocks of wood (½" x ½" x 8½"), glued in the dado channels cut into the sides of the drawers. When finished, the drawers are slid into the cabinet so that the guide rails fit into the side and divider dado channels. In time and with the aid of candle wax or soap, the drawers will slide easily.

Attach the two front pieces. A piano hinge is used for the bottom door, and two butt hinges are used for the top door. Careful alignment is necessary for a flush fit. Attach a hasp where the two edges of the front meet. Attach a concealed handle to each side.

The camp kitchen should be finished with an exterior grade paint on all surfaces. Keep in mind the fact that bright, light colors tend to attract flies and other insects, while darker colors do not. Internal surfaces can be finished with paint or a clear coating such as polyurethane. You might consider staining interior surfaces before applying a clear finish.

UTILITY TRAILER

A small utility trailer is very handy for the outdoorsman, rancher, farmer, or handyman. While several companies sell small trailers in both assembled and kit form, the handy outdoorsman can make one quite easily from plywood, angle iron, an automotive axle from the local auto junk yard, and a trailer hitch tongue.

The dimensions for this utility trailer are the size of a sheet of ¾" CDX plywood, 4' x 8'. The sides can vary in height from no sides to 4' high, but a 2' height is best for all-around use, and will enable you to haul up to one-half a cord of firewood easily.

Materials List

▼▼▼▼▼▼▼▼▼▼▼▼▼▼▼▼▼▼▼▼▼▼▼▼

¾" CDX plywood (three sheets required)
1" x 1" steel angle iron: 75'
Rear axle with leaf springs, rims, and tires
2" x 2" steel tubing: 6'
Trailer hitch tongue

▼▼

Cut the angle iron to form a frame which measures 4' x 8' and into which a full sheet of plywood will fit snugly. The frame can be bolted together but will be much stronger if the joints can be welded. If you do not have welding equipment or the skills required, consider having the work done at a professional welding shop.

Weld the trailer tongue and hitch to the frame. Bolt the leaf springs and axle to the frame. If you want sides on the trailer, cut and attach the uprights, one at each corner and spaced about 2' along the sides, and top rails. These pieces should also be welded. Some cutting and fitting will be required. Next, cut and fit the ¾" plywood side panels. These must be attached with screws after drilling the angle iron frame at suitable locations.

The final step is to prime all wood and metal surfaces. Keep in mind that a metal primer should be used for the angle iron frame and tongue, but do not paint the leaf springs or axle. After the primer has dried, paint the entire trailer with a good grade exterior paint.

One worthwhile addition to your small utility trailer is to attach eye bolts around the sides of the unit. These will enable you to tie down a tarp to help keep things secured while traveling at highway speeds.

In many states, a light utility trailer does not require directional, stop, or running lights. Check with your state's department of motor vehicles. If they are, they can be purchased from an automotive supply store along with the necessary wire. Registration may also be required in your state, so be sure to check before using.

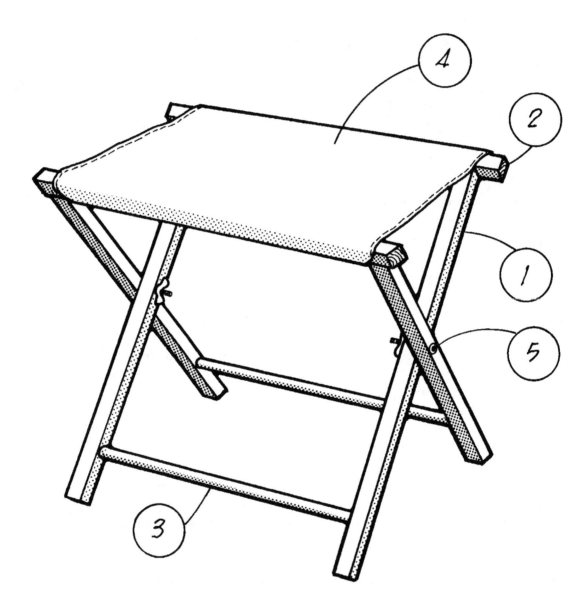

A comfortable place to sit while on a camping trip can be difficult to find but the following project can easily solve the problem. In addition, the folding camp seat takes up very little room when traveling and will support a large adult safely. The lumber used for the camp seat should be hardwood. Some of the better choices include ash, maple, cherry, and white oak. Purchase the lumber in a full 1" x 6" size, then rip the pieces as indicated. There will be some waste lumber after the cutting.

Materials List
▼▼▼▼▼▼▼▼▼▼▼▼▼▼▼▼▼▼▼▼▼▼▼▼

1. Legs: 1" x 1" x 19" (four required)
2. Top rails: one 1" x 1" x 15", one 1" x 1" x 13"
3. Bottom rails: ⅝" dowel, one 13½", one 11½"
4. Canvas: 11" x 24"
5. Bolts: two 3", two wing nuts and six washers

▼▼

Using a table saw if available, cut the lumber to the dimensions shown in the materials list. Drill out the holes in the legs for the bottom rails, 2" up from the bottom edge and ¼" deep. Use a ⅝" spade or Forstner bit. Then drill the top rails to receive the legs, ¾" holes, 1⅛" in from each end, ½" deep. Drill holes through the legs for the bolts, 10" up from the bottom of each leg.

The top of each of the four legs must be trimmed to fit into the ¾" holes in the top rail. This is most easily done with a wood carving knife or wood rasp. Work carefully to carve the leg tops so they will fit ½" into the ¾" diameter holes in the top rails.

Fit the dowels into the bottom leg sections using construction adhesive. The two inner legs use the shorter dowel and the two outer legs receive the longer dowel. Fit the top of the legs into the top rails, also using construction adhesive. Bolt the legs together, placing a washer on the outside, between, and on the inside of the legs, and fasten with a wing nut.

It is a good idea to finish the woodwork before attaching the canvas. Sand as required, then apply two coats of varnish or polyurethane. As a rule, two light coats of the clear finish are better than one heavy coat.

Once the clear finish has dried, wrap one end of the canvas around the top rail and staple in place on the outside of the rail using ⅜" staples. Partially fold the seat closed and wrap the free end of the canvas around the other top rail and staple.

CHAPTER 3
HUNTING & FISHING PROJECTS
▼▼

Homemade duck decoys are just as effective as commercially made decoys and can be made for a fraction of the price.

More ducks can be bagged if they can be lured into shotgun range. As a result of this knowledge, duck decoys have been made and used by duck hunters for centuries. Proof of the duck decoy's longevity was established in the early 1920s when a dozen hand-made decoys were discovered under a pile of 1,000-year-old debris in Nevada's Lovelock Cave. These decoys were perfectly preserved in the dry climate, and are assumed to have been used by American Indians to lure ducks into rock and arrow range.

Over time, different materials have been used to make duck decoys with varying degrees of success. The major flyways, migration routes of ducks and geese, of the United States have been the areas where the best duck hunting can be found during the fall and early winter, and not surprisingly, these are also the areas where hunters produced the most effective decoys.

The Atlantic Flyway, a broad band stretching from Maine to the Carolinas, is probably the best example of a part of the United States that has produced more than its share of decoy makers and decoys for waterfowl. Narraganset Bay, the Great South Bay, and Barnegat Bay are three areas that have been the home of some of the most famous and best decoy makers.

Today, decoys made in these areas command high prices from antique dealers and collectors. At an auction in 1986, a pair of hand-carved merganser diving ducks was sold for $93,000. At that same auction, a preening pintail decoy sold for a record $319,000.

Modern duck hunters have learned that the best way to lure ducks into shotgun range is to use realistic decoys. A number of companies make duck and goose decoys, but the price can be prohibitive, especially for those just starting out. At this time, one dozen plastic-bodied mallard duck decoys costs around $60. Hand-made cork duck decoys cost $25 to $50 each.

A wide variety of materials can be used to make duck decoys including cork, cedar, pine, and Styrofoam. Unfortunately, cork in 2" thick sheet form is very difficult to find. Many decoy makers feel that this is the best material for working (floating) duck decoys. Cedar and pine blocks 4" high by 12" long are available as fence posts, but require quite a bit of woodworking before effective-looking floating decoys can be made. Therefore, the best material, from the standpoint of availability and work required per decoy, is Styrofoam.

Materials List
▼▼▼▼▼▼▼▼▼▼▼▼▼▼▼▼▼▼▼▼▼▼

Styrofoam insulation: 2" x 24" x 8' (two required for 12 decoys)
Redwood: 2" x 6" x 4', clear heart or construction heart
Wooden dowel: ¾", 6'
Lumber: 1" x 4" x 8'
Panel and foam adhesive (two tubes)
Decoy paint kit
Finishing nails: 6d and 4d as required
Tire wheel weights: twelve as required for keel weights
Decoy anchor line as required, and twelve one-ounce sinkers

▼▼

Styrofoam insulation, in 2" x 24" sheets, is sold in home improvement centers. Two or more layers of this material must be sandwiched together with waterproof foam panel adhesive applied between the layers to achieve the proper height of a decoy body. A good rule of thumb is that the block must be at least 4" thick and 6" wide. The decoy body should be at least 11" long before shaping.

Once the adhesive has sets fully—overnight is best—saw the block of Styrofoam into a rough decoy body shape. Use the silhouette illustration as a rough guide. Next, shape it with a rasp or surform tool until a rough likeness of a duck body is achieved. Follow this by sanding lightly to achieve smooth lines.

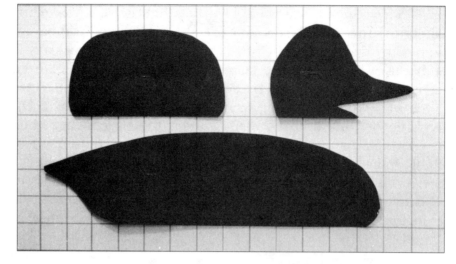

Silhouette of diver duck on 1" grid.

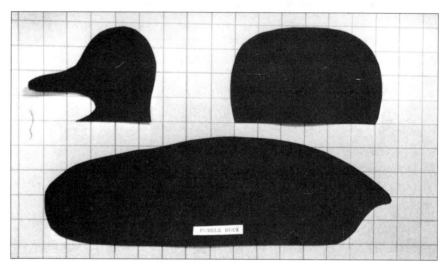

Silhouette of puddle duck on 1" grid.

To make a decoy head, trace the pattern on the 2" x 6" redwood lumber. Straight-grained lumber without any knots is best. Specify clear heart or construction heart redwood. The pattern should be traced so that the grain runs horizontally with the bill of the head. Cut the head out. Use a saber saw or band saw, if available. Shape the head with the aid of a rasp or surform tool. A sharp wood carving knife can also be used. After the head has been roughed out, hand sanding will help to smooth and finish it off.

Once the head has been shaped, drill a ¾" hole approximately 1½" into the bottom and glue a ¾" diameter dowel, 6" long, in place. This dowel will be used to fasten the head to the decoy body. You may also want to drive a 4d finishing nail to further secure the head to the dowel. If you do this, drill a hole first, then countersink the nail head in place.

Attach a length of 1x4 pine flat to the bottom of the decoy body. Taper both ends and fasten it in place with waterproof adhesive. Taper the ends of the

1x4 to conceal this material from view when it is floating. The tapered 1x4 will also add strength to the decoy and offer a suitable location for a keel weight if needed for level floatation.

▼▼▼▼▼▼▼▼▼▼▼▼▼▼▼▼▼▼▼▼▼▼

Styrofoam is shaped into a duck decoy bottom with hand tools.

▲▲▲▲▲▲▲▲▲▲▲▲▲▲▲▲▲▲▲▲▲▲▲

▼▼▼▼▼▼▼▼▼▼▼▼▼▼▼▼▼▼▼▼▼

Use a rasp for shaping a duck decoy head.

▲▲▲▲▲▲▲▲▲▲▲▲▲▲▲▲▲▲▲▲▲▲▲

Drill a ¾" hole through the decoy body and 1x4, at the location of the head. Apply waterproof construction adhesive liberally along the dowel, then press the decoy head and dowel through the hole. Position the head so that the bill is facing forward. Drive a 6d finishing nail through the edge of the 1x4 and dowel to help secure the dowel.

Once the adhesive has dried, cut off the end of the wooden dowel so that it is flush with the bottom of the 1x4. Drill a hole horizontally through the 1x4 so that a decoy anchor line can be attached in this concealed location.

Test the decoy in water to see how it floats. Often, because Styrofoam is so light, the decoy will not float properly. If so, fasten a tire wheel weight to the 1x4 on the bottom of decoy. Experiment to achieve a natural float. If you are planning to use your decoys in a field, rather than as floaters, the weight can be eliminated.

▼▼▼▼▼▼▼▼▼▼▼▼▼▼▼▼▼▼▼▼▼

Attach the decoy head through the body.

▲▲▲▲▲▲▲▲▲▲▲▲▲▲▲▲▲▲▲▲▲

The last step is to paint the duck decoy to closely resemble the species of duck you will be trying to lure into shotgun range. Purchase a decoy paint kit at a sporting goods store or through outdoor equipment mail order catalogs. Buy the kit for a given type of duck—mallard, scalp, goldeneye, black duck— and you will get both the required paints and a painting chart showing how to realistically paint both hens and drakes.

When using a decoy, attach 6' (minimum) of anchor line to the bottom of the decoy. Then attach a one-ounce sinker to the other end. This arrangement should hold your decoys where you put them even in the strongest winds.

CANADA GOOSE SILHOUETTE DECOYS ———

Goose hunting is not for the faint of heart or those who are not long on patience. Usually the big migrations of Canada geese do not start until the weather up north begins to take a turn for the worse. But once the major migrations begin, large numbers of these birds can usually be lured into properly set up stands of decoys. As a rule of thumb, the more goose decoys you can set out, the better your chances of attracting large flocks to within shotgun range.

Serious goose hunters commonly set out from four to ten dozen Canada goose decoys and usually wish they had more when the geese start flying. Commercially made full-bodied goose decoys cost around $60 per dozen. As you can see, it is easy to invest quite a few dollars just to get started in goose hunting. In addition, a dozen Canada goose decoys will weigh about twenty pounds and, because they are bulky, just carrying a few dozen decoys out to a goose hunting blind can be quite an undertaking.

The do-it-yourself woodworker outdoorsman can easily make several dozen full-size Canada goose silhouette decoys, using ½" CDX plywood, in just a few hours. Silhouette goose decoys are light and, because each is only ½" thick, are not bulky, so are easy to carry. When set up properly, silhouette goose decoys are just as effective as full-bodied goose decoys.

Most goose hunting experts agree that a typical stand of decoys should contain one sentry for every five feeder geese. A sentry has an upright head while the necks of feeders are bent toward the ground. Approximately twelve goose decoys can be cut from a single sheet of plywood. Make two templates out of cardboard, based on the illustration.

Materials List

▼▼▼▼▼▼▼▼▼▼▼▼▼▼▼▼▼▼▼▼▼▼▼▼▼

For one dozen goose decoys:

½" CDX plywood: one sheet
Galvanized wire: 10-gauge, 18'
Flat black exterior paint: one gallon
Flat white exterior paint: one pint
Flat brown exterior paint: one pint

▼▼

Trace the outlines of both sentries and feeder geese on a sheet of plywood. Make a cardboard template of both types from the silhouette illustration, then use these to help you lay out the outlines on the plywood. Cut out the silhouettes, using a saber or bayonet saw. Use a plywood blade for smooth cuts. Sand each smooth, paying careful attention to the edges.

▼▼▼▼▼▼▼▼▼▼▼▼▼▼▼▼▼▼▼▼▼▼

Silhouette of Canada goose sentry on 1" grid.

▲▲▲▲▲▲▲▲▲▲▲▲▲▲▲▲▲▲▲▲▲▲▲▲

Paint all silhouettes flat black, both sides including the edges. A good grade exterior latex paint works best. When this dries, apply flat white exterior paint for cheek slashes and just below the tail. Again, when the paint is dry, paint the body and wings in a flat, brown color.

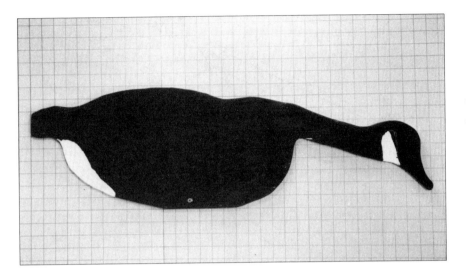

▼▼▼▼▼▼▼▼▼▼▼▼▼▼▼▼▼▼▼▼

Silhouette of Canada goose feeder on 1" grid.

▲▲▲▲▲▲▲▲▲▲▲▲▲▲▲▲▲▲▲▲▲▲▲

Drill a ⅛" hole, 2" up from the bottom and centered on the body. When setting up these decoys in the field, push an 18" length of 10-gauge galvanized wire through this hole and bend it in half to act as two stabilizing legs. Push these legs down into the soil to both conceal the legs and to add stability in the wind. To add more realism to your goose decoys, remove wings from downed birds and staple these to the decoys.

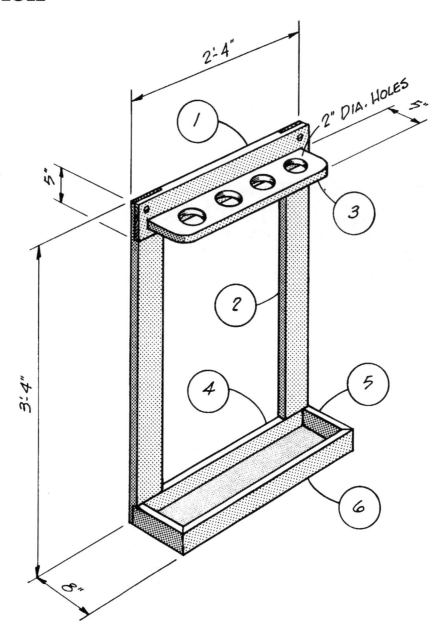

In this day and age, when burglaries are rampant, it is almost inconceivable that anyone would keep firearms displayed in the open. Nevertheless, there are certain instances when a rifle rack by the door is both practical and a good idea. One example is a cabin in a rural area that is used during the hunting season. It is much safer to rack firearms than to stack them around a cabin.

A rifle rack can be as simple as pegs on a wall or as classic as a glass-fronted cabinet. (A gun cabinet project is covered later in this chapter.) For all practical purposes a four-gun rack, where rifles or shotguns can be stored upright, should be suitable for almost any hunting cabin.

Materials List

1. Top rail: 1" x 5" x 28"
2. Side rails: 1" x 3" x 3' 4" long (two required)
3. Top front: 1" x 5" x 26"
4. Front and back of base: 1" x 2" x 28" (two required)
5. Ends of base: 1" x 2" x 8" (two required)
6. Bottom of base: ¾" CDX plywood, 6½" x 26½"
   One tube construction adhesive
   Twelve #8 wood screws 1" long,
   Green felt for lining the base and barrel cut-out holes
   One quart clear finish
   One pint stain
   Four #12 wood screws 3" long or two toggle bolts for mounting
   4d finishing nails as required

The rifle rack shown in the illustration is made from white or red oak but other hardwoods could, of course, be substituted. Cut the pieces as indicated in the materials list. Dado cut the ends of the top section (1) and the top ends of the side rails (2), (⅜" deep by 5" wide). The bottom of the side rails should also be dado cut ⅜" deep and 2" wide. Drill 2" diameter holes in the top front piece (3) and round off the front edges. Attach the top front piece to the top section, using construction adhesive and inserting screws from behind.

Build the base by assembling parts 4, 5, and 6. Use construction adhesive and 4d finishing nails, countersinking the heads. Attach the top rail to the side rails, then attach the base to the side rails, also using construction adhesive and screws through the base to the side rails. When using oak, it is often necessary to predrill the screw holes to prevent splitting.

Finish the gun rack with stain and clear finish. After finish dries, line the holes in the top front with strips of felt. Line the bottom of base with felt. Mount rack to wall, using wood screws and/or toggle bolts if required.

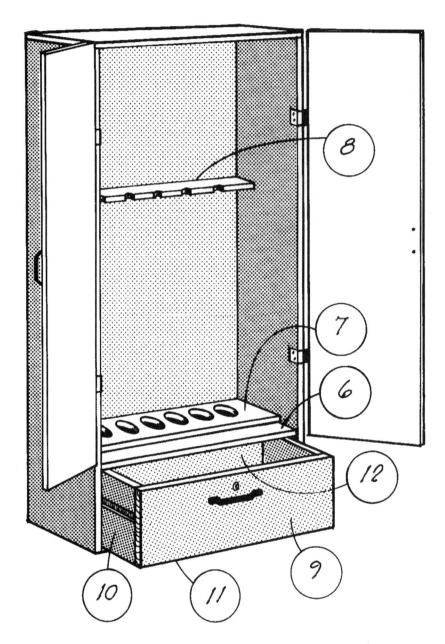

As mentioned earlier, it is almost inconceivable that anyone would store firearms in a glass-fronted cabinet in the home where they could easily be taken by a burglar. The plywood doors on the project in this section will keep your rifles and shotguns out of sight. Location certainly plays an important part—both the location of your home, relative to high crime areas, and location in the home of the firearms cabinet itself. Most crime experts suggest that firearms should be stored on upper and lower floors of the home rather than on the main floor.

Nevertheless, if you feel your home is in a low crime area and if you have a suitable location in your home for a gun cabinet, such a piece of furniture is functional and an attractive addition. A den or recreation room could be an ideal setting for a gun cabinet, for example. A good gun cabinet is one that can be locked. While this will obviously not stop a determined burglar, a lock on the gun cabinet door will discourage children or unauthorized people from touching your firearms.

The illustration shows a six-gun cabinet which is made almost entirely of ¾" shop-grade plywood. There are a number of different hardwood veneers available including oak, cherry, maple, birch, and mahogany. Choose a face veneer that will enhance your stored firearms as well as complement your existing furniture.

Materials List
▼▼▼▼▼▼▼▼▼▼▼▼▼▼▼▼▼▼▼▼▼▼▼▼▼▼

Cut from ¾" AB interior plywood except as noted. Three sheets required

1. Top: 20" x 36"
2. Sides: 20" x 72" (two required)
3. Back: 36" x 72"—¼" Masonite
4. Bottom: 20" x 34½"
5. Doors: 18" x 60" (two required)
6. Divider: 20" x 34½"
7. Rifle base holder: 10" x 34½"
8. Barrel holder: 3½" x 34½"
9. Drawer front: 11¼" x 34½"
10. Drawer sides: 11" x 18½" (two required)
11. Drawer bottom: 17" x 34½", Masonite
12. Drawer back: 11" x 34½"
    Drawer guide rails: ½" x ½" x 18" pine, (two required)
13. Hardware:
    Handles: three 4"
    Hinges: four, concealed type
    Locks, keyed alike: two (disc tumbler cam type)
    Wood filler paste, stain, clear finish, felt, construction adhesive
    4d and 6d finishing nails

Mark and cut all materials based on the materials list. A table saw is best for straight cuts or use a hand-held circular saw with an edge guide. Then make dado channel cuts (¼" deep, ½" wide) to the two drawer sides, 6" up from the bottom edge. Also make dado channel cuts 6¾" up from the bottom of both sides of the cabinet. Install the ½" x ½" x 18" drawer guide rails into the dado grooves in the cabinet sides. Use construction adhesive and 4d finishing nails.

Assemble the cabinet in the following order: Attach the sides to the bottom, then the top to the sides. Use 6d finishing nails and construction adhesive for all joints. Next, attach the back to the unit. This will add much stability to the unit. The divider is next to be installed, and placement is important. The divider should be located 12" up from the bottom of the cabinet. Mark the location first, then install with construction adhesive and 6d finishing nails.

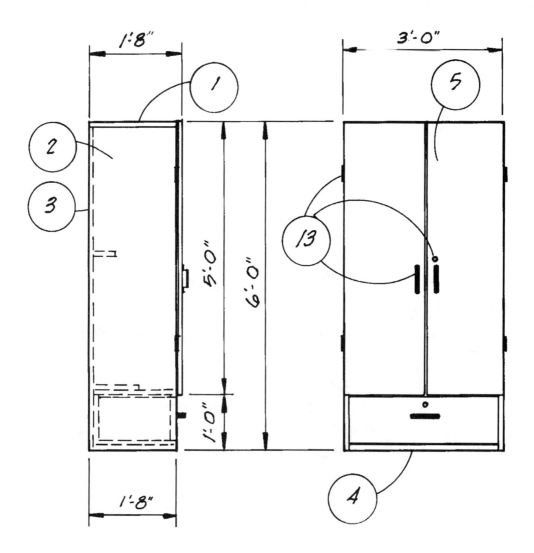

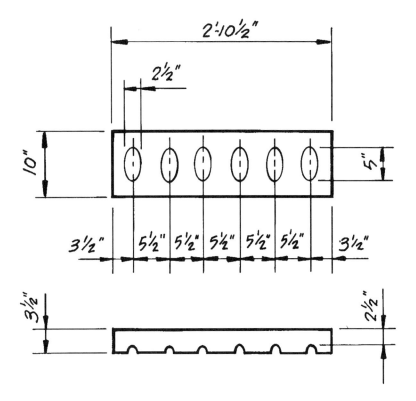

The rifle base should be carefully marked and the holes cut. A saber saw or router can be used for this task. Install the base on top of the divider, using construction adhesive and nailing through the sides of the cabinet.

Next, make the cut-outs on the barrel holder. Mark the location of the barrel holder inside the cabinet, 24" down from the top, and install using construction adhesive and finishing nails driven in from the outside of the cabinet.

Build the drawer by assembling the parts using construction adhesive and 6d finishing nails. Use 4d finishing nails for attaching the Masonite bottom. Once constructed, the drawer should slide into place on the drawer guidance rails located inside the cabinet. An application of soap or candle wax to the guide rails will make the drawer slide with ease.

Carefully cut the two doors and install with concealed hinges to the inside of the cabinet.

All exposed nail heads should be filled with a paste filler and the entire cabinet sanded before a finish coating is applied. If a wood stain is used, let it dry before applying two coats of clear finish.

Allow ample time for the finish to dry, then apply felt strips to the cut-outs in the barrel holder, and inside rifle base slots. Lastly, attach the handles and locks to the drawer and doors.

FLY TYER'S MATERIALS CASE

If you are a serious fly tyer, you have probably acquired a large selection of fly tying materials—hooks, thread, tools, feathers, furs, and a variety of other materials. Chances are also good that these materials are stored in airtight boxes around your home. Having these materials close at hand makes sense, but often from a practical point of view, this is just not possible. A fly tyer's materials case can solve a lot of your organizational problems because all of the commonly used tools and materials can be contained in one case.

Materials List

▼▼▼▼▼▼▼▼▼▼▼▼▼▼▼▼▼▼▼▼▼▼▼▼▼

All parts from ½" AB plywood, except as noted. One-half sheet required.

1. Top of lid: 9" x 14"
2. & 3. Front and back of lid: 2" x 15" (two required)
4. Sides of lid: 2" x 9" (two required)
5. Sides of box: 9½" x 14" (two required)
6. Back of box: 14" x 14"
7. Front of box: 4" x 15"
8. Door: 10" x 15"
9. Bottom of box: 9½" x 14"
10. Bottom of top compartment: 9" x 14"
11. Piano hinge: 15" long (two required)
12. Handle: 4"
13. Latches: (three required)

Bottom Drawer
Face and back: 3½" x 14"
Sides: 3½" x 8" (two required)
Bottom: 8½" x 14½" *
Drawer guide rails: ½" x ½" x 8" (six required)

Two Top Drawers
3" x 14" (four required)
3" x 8" (four required)
8½" x 14½" (two required*)

Also required: one tube construction adhesive, 4d finishing nails, wood filler paste, one-half pint stain, one quart polyurethane finish.

* ¼" Masonite

▼▼

Begin by cutting all parts based on materials list description. Next make dado channels, ¼" deep and ½" wide, on the insides of the cabinet. These are located 2", 6" and 8½" up from the bottom of both side pieces. Once these channels have been cut, install the drawer guide rails, using construction adhesive and 4d finishing nails. The drawer guide rails should be located ½" in from both the front and back edges.

Make a ¼" deep dado cut ½" up from the bottom on the inside of all drawer pieccs so the Masonite bottoms can be inserted. Then make dado channel cuts, ¼" deep and ½" wide, on the outside of all drawer side pieccs. These dado cuts are part of the drawer guidance system and are located 1½" up from the bottom of all sides and the ends of the back pieces.

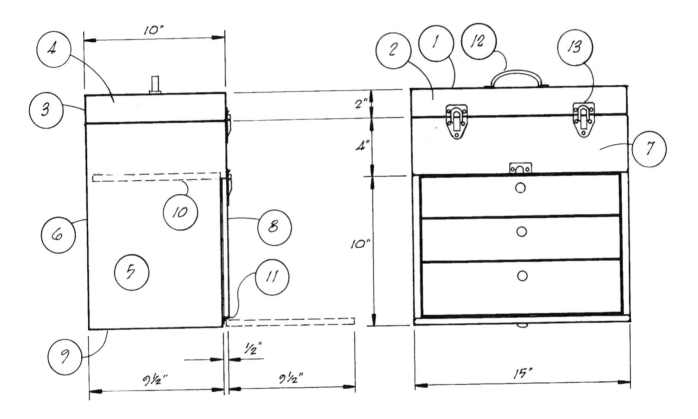

Bore a ¾" hole in the center of the three drawer faces. These holes serve as finger pulls to open the drawers. Use a ¾" spade or Forstner bit for a clean hole.

Build the top section first by assembling parts #1, 2, 3, and 4. Use construction adhesive and 4d finishing nails. Attach the face and back to the top, then attach the sides.

Next build the cabinet by assembling sides (5), bottom (9), back (6) and front (7). Use construction adhesive and finishing nails. Attach lid to cabinet with one piano hinge. Attach the front door with the other piano hinge. Attach handle to top and latches to face. Note that one latch secures the door while the other two latches are for the lid.

Assemble the drawers with construction adhesive and 4d finishing nails. You will find the assembly easier if you attach the back to the sides first, insert the Masonite bottom piece, then attach the front of the drawer by nailing through the face into the ends of the sides. The drawers should slide easily onto the guide rails which were installed on the sides of the cabinet earlier. The addition of candle wax or soap to the guide rails will make the drawers slide smoothly.

Countersink and fill all nail holes with paste filler material and sand flush when dry. Sand all surfaces smooth before applying stain. Apply two light coats of polyurethane to all surfaces, allowing sufficient drying time between coats.

INLAID WOODEN RIFLE STOCK ———————————

Firearm stocks have been decorated in a variety of ways for centuries, and now there is a revival, especially for fine firearms. While some embellishments such as engravings and gold inlays are out of the realm of the do-it-yourselfer, inlays of exotic woods to the stocks of rifles and shotguns and pistol grips can be done by the careful craftsman. What's more, if these inlays are done carefully, they will enhance the beauty of the firearm and could add to its value.

At least part of the success at inlaying a rifle stock lies in exact planning of the design. Draw the design on paper before transferring it to a stock. Both the design and its location on the stock should be carefully considered. Keep in mind that a simple design is usually best and most easily done by the amateur. Shapes such as a diamond are usually well within the capabilities of most and can easily be done with simple woodworking tools.

The beginner should make a practice inlay before carving up a favorite rifle stock. Once you have mastered cutting and fitting the inlay, you can make an inlay on a rifle stock with a much greater chance of success.

▼▼

Gather together the inlay pattern, hardwood veneer material, and a piece of scrap hardwood lumber.

Trace the outline of the inlay onto the scrap lumber. Use a sharp tool such as a metal scribe. After the pattern has been carefully transferred to the scrap hardwood lumber, begin carving the outline with a sharp chisel. Use a mallet to tap the chisel down to a depth which is just slightly less than the thickness of the veneer inlay. Once the outline of the design has been cut, carve out the interior of the pattern with the wood chisel. Hand wood-carving tools are very useful for this type of detail carving.

After the inlay pattern has been cut—to a depth which is just slightly less than the thickness of the veneer—it is time to cut and fit the inlay. Begin by tracing the design onto the face of the veneer and then cut, using a sharp razor knife. Next, lay the cut veneer into the inlay area. Some trimming of the veneer may be required. Once you are satisfied with the fit of the inlay, apply casin glue to the back of the piece and press it in place. Clamp the inlay in place for at least four hours, overnight is better.

Once the adhesive has set fully, remove the clamp and sand the inlay flush with the surrounding area. Use a fine grit sandpaper—200 grit or higher—to avoid damaging the veneer.

Once you have mastered the art of tracing and cutting inlays on scrap material, you can try your hand at making an inlay in a favorite rifle stock.

Work carefully when inlaying veneer on a favorite rifle stock. All of the steps are the same as with the practice inlay. Once you have completed the inlay, the stock must be finished properly.

After sanding the inlay flush with the surrounding area, apply two or more coats of a stock finishing liquid, which is commonly available from sporting goods stores that carry a line of firearm accessory items.

Two good sources of veneer for inlaying are: The Woodworkers' Store, 21801 Industrial Boulevard, Rogers, MN 55374-9514, and Constantine, 2056 Eastchester Road, Bronx, NY 10461.

OUTDOOR ARCHERY RANGE
(Backstop)

Archery has become increasingly popular in the United States over the past decade. Changes in equipment design and materials used have resulted in compound bows and arrows that are both powerful and accurate. Many hunters find bow hunting to be much more challenging than rifle hunting. As a result, they choose archery as a means of bagging big game animals.

A modern compound bow is extremely accurate. Many believe that a bow is at least as accurate as a large caliber pistol at comparable ranges. A variety of sighting devices is available that make shooting a bow easier than ever before. Nevertheless, before an archer can feel confident about placing an arrow in the bull's-eye, many hours of practice are required. Target shooting is possible in most backyards providing suitable targets and backstops are available. Only after hours of practice can an archer expect to develop the skills needed to draw a bow and release an arrow properly.

Bow hunters have come up with a variety of interesting targets for practice. Probably the most popular is several bales of hay and a sand pile. Commercially made fiber or foam targets are also available, and these types do less damage to arrow shafts.

A perfectly suitable target can easily be made by with polyethylene foam in sheet form. Polyethylene foam is a closed-cell, dense foam that has a tendency to reseal itself after punctures. It is available in 2' x 2' squares, 2 or more inches thick. The best archery targets are made by laminating two 2" layers of the foam together and backing them with a 2' x 2' square of CDX plywood.

Materials List
▼▼▼▼▼▼▼▼▼▼▼▼▼▼▼▼▼▼▼▼▼▼▼▼▼▼

1. One sheet ½" thick CDX plywood, 2' x 2' square
2. Two sheets polyethylene foam, 2' x 2' square, 2" thick
3. Three pieces 2x2 pine, 6' long
4. One 6" long bolt, four washers, one wing nut
   One tube foam and panel adhesive
   One pint each red, yellow, and black exterior paint
   6d finishing nails as required

▼▼

Laminate the two pieces of foam together using foam adhesive. Then laminate the foam target to the plywood back. Lay the foam and plywood flat and place a weight on top to keep the two together while the adhesive sets properly—overnight is best, but four hours should suffice if you are in a hurry.

Drill a ⅜" hole, one inch down from the top of each of the three legs. Using panel adhesive and 6d finishing nails, attach two of the legs to the back of the target panel. The top of the third leg must fit between the tops of the other legs and be secured with the bolt, washers, and wing nut.

To use the target, spread the legs to form a tripod. Tighten the wing nut to hold the legs in that position. On the face of the target you can either paint a three ring bull's-eye or use a paper target. In time you will have to replace the center of the target. Cut out a square larger than the bull's-eye and replace with two new pieces of polyethylene foam.

INDOOR BB GUN RANGE
(Backstop)

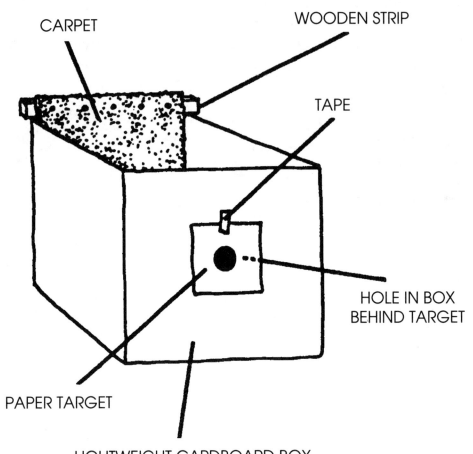

CARPET

WOODEN STRIP

TAPE

HOLE IN BOX
BEHIND TARGET

PAPER TARGET

LIGHTWEIGHT CARDBOARD BOX

Using BB and pellet guns, you can develop your shooting skills without the noise, expense, or potential danger of conventional firearms. Many shooting experts agree that the basics of firearm handling and shooting should be taught to youngsters with the aid of BB guns. As the child progresses, learning safety and skill, he can move on to a small caliber firearm with continued adult supervision.

Safe shooting practices begin by only shooting at a safe target. A perfectly safe and suitable BB backstop can be made from a large cardboard box and a scrap of carpeting.

Materials List

▼▼▼▼▼▼▼▼▼▼▼▼▼▼▼▼▼▼▼▼▼▼▼▼▼

Cardboard box—new appliance box, for example
Indoor/outdoor carpeting—enough to cover the back of box
2x2 lumber: one 4' length
Panel adhesive, staple gun, 9/16" staples as required.

▼▼

Get a large cardboard box, a TV or major appliance box works well. Remove the top of the box with a razor knife. Attach a piece of carpeting to a length of 2x2 lumber, a stapler works well for this. The lumber extends across the top of the box and holds the piece of carpeting behind the target area. The carpeting should be as wide as the box.

Cut a hole in the front center of the box slightly smaller than the size of your paper target. Tape the target over the hole and your indoor BB gun range is ready for use.

Be sure to place the target in a safe area, indoors or out. The carpeting will stop BB's, and allow you to collect them for reshooting.

LIVE BAIT BOX

A live bait box is handy for fishing where minnows or other bait fish are used, particularly when fishing from a boat in either fresh or salt water. It will keep minnows fresh and lively for several days if the box is allowed to float in water. Along coastal areas, large floating bait boxes are used by bait dealers to store bait fish throughout the season.

A good size is 6" wide, 19½" long, and 6" deep. Almost any scrap lumber can be used. Plywood must be the marine grade type. The top should be easy to remove and is commonly held in place with a wooden or metal turnbuckle. The bottom should be covered with hardware cloth with ¼" to ½" mesh to allow fresh water to circulate in and out of the box.

Materials List

▼▼▼▼▼▼▼▼▼▼▼▼▼▼▼▼▼▼▼▼▼▼▼▼▼

Ends: 1" x 6" x 6" (two required)
Sides: 1" x 6" x 18" (two required)
Top: 1" x 6" x 19½", cut into three equal pieces
    two 1" x 2" x 4" strips for bottom of lid
Turnbuckle: metal or 1" x 2" x 3" strip, 2" bolt, nut and washer
Hardware cloth: 7" x 20" with ⅛" mesh
Nylon cord, 6'
Large screw-eye bolt
Staple gun, galvanized 6d finishing nails, and waterproof construction
    adhesive

▼▼▼

Cut the pieces according to the materials list. Attach the end pieces to the sides using waterproof construction adhesive and 6d finishing nails. Nail two top pieces to the box, one on each end in the same manner. Nail the two wooden strips on the underside of the third top piece so they will be concealed when the lid is in place. Insert the center top piece in place. Install the turn buckle to one of the top pieces so that it will secure the middle top piece when turned. Fit the hardware cloth to the bottom of the box. Some trimming of the cloth may be required. Staple the hardware cloth to the bottom of the box.

The box can be painted, a color to match your boat, for example, or left natural. Attach the screw eye bolt to one end of the box and tie on one end of the nylon cord. This live bait is designed for still fishing from the shore, a dock, or while in a boat. In use, live bait fish are placed in the box and it is allowed to float close at hand.

FISHING ROD RACK

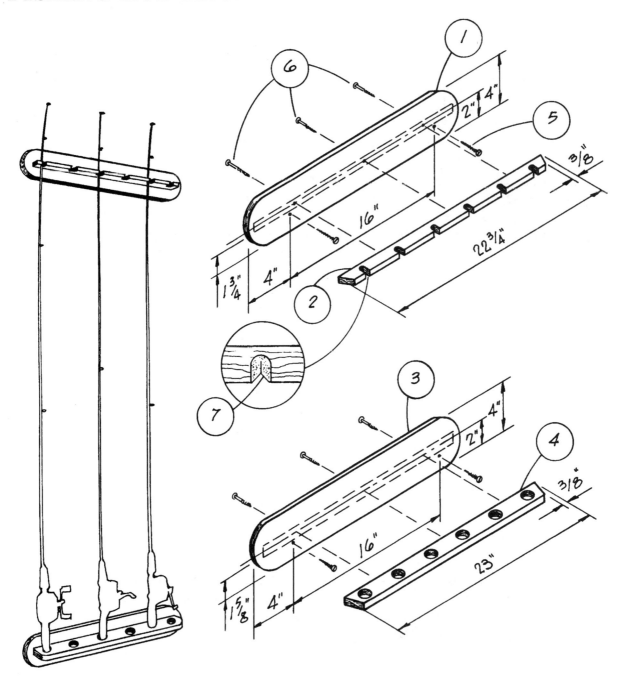

F ishing rods have a tendency to end up in a corner of the garage or basement when not in use. As a result, when it comes time to go fishing, the trip usually begins with untangling a mass of fiberglass, monofilament line, and hooks. One good way to avoid this hassle is to build a fishing rod rack for storing your rods. The money you save not having to replace broken rods will more than pay for the materials.

Materials List
▼▼▼▼▼▼▼▼▼▼▼▼▼▼▼▼▼▼▼▼▼▼▼

(All parts cut from oak, maple, or cherry) one each 1" x 6" x 24" and 1" x 8" x 24" required

1. Top mounting board: 4" x 24"
2. Top retainer strip: 1¾" x 22¾"
3. Bottom mounting board: 4" x 24"
4. Bottom shelf: 3" x 23"
5. Wall mounting screws or toggle bolts: 3" (four required)
6. Strip mounting screws: 1¼" (six required)
7. Foam strips for top retainer strip: ¾" x 2" (six required)
    Polyvinyl resin adhesive, 6d finishing nails, stain, clear finish

▼▼▼

Cut the pieces according to the materials list. If you want a decorative edge to the top and bottom mounting boards use a router equipped with a Roman ogee bit. If not, round off all edges with sandpaper. Make ¾" cutouts (as indicated) on the top retainer strip. Use a Forstner drill bit and a saber saw for the cutouts. Next mark and drill 1½" holes part way through into the bottom shelf. A hole saw, which chucks into an electric drill is the right tool for these holes.

After all pieces have been cut, sand them well. This will make finishing later much easier.

Join the top retainer strip to the top mounting board. Drill holes for screws. Apply a bead of polyvinyl resin adhesive before mating surfaces then screw two pieces together. Fasten the bottom shelf to the bottom mounting board in the same way.

The fishing rod rack is ready for finishing. Lightly sand all pieces, then apply wood stain. Apply two light coats of clear finish such as varnish or polyurethane, allowing the pieces to dry overnight before applying the second coat.

After the finish has dried, install the strips of foam into the cut outs on the top retainer strip. Use adhesive and trim the foam flush with the openings if necessary.

Mount the two boards on the wall, using a level to get them plumb. Use screws or toggle bolts through the face of both pieces. Space them about 4' apart. Once wall mounted, the fishing rod rack is ready for service, and the next time you get ready to go fishing, you will know exactly where your rods are.

AMMUNITION RELOADING BENCH ———
(with Powder Locker)

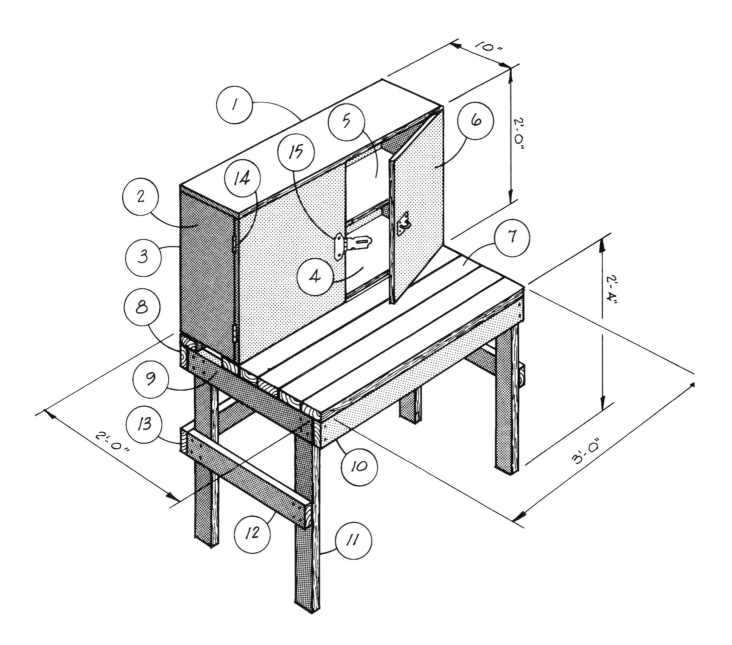

Ammunition reloading is increasing in popularity in the United States for a variety of reasons, not the least of which is inexpensive ammunition that is equal to or better than ammunition made by the major manufacturers. Quality ammunition can be reloaded at home for about one-fourth the price of commercially manufactured ammunition If you are a hunter or shooter, this translates into more bang for your bucks.

To be sure, an investment in equipment is required. A reloading press, one set of dies, a scale, a book containing reloading data, and a few other tools are needed. In addition you must purchase primers, powder, and bullets. The shotgun reloader must buy powder, wads, shot, and primers. You also need empty brass or shotshells for the reloading. Other than these basic tools and components, the only other thing required is a stout workbench to hold the press.

A powder locker is a good addition for a reloading bench. The cabinet need not be large but it should have a hasp and lock so powder, primers, and other dangerous materials can be secured.

A suitable size reloading bench can be constructed entirely from 2x4s, but the bench will be stronger if larger dimensional lumber such as 2x6 or 2x8 boards are used for the top. If a 2x4 top is used, cover it with ¼" Masonite to prevent small parts from falling between the boards.

Materials List
▼▼▼▼▼▼▼▼▼▼▼▼▼▼▼▼▼▼▼▼▼▼▼▼▼▼

One sheet ¾" AB plywood, four 8' and three 6' 2x4s
1. Top of locker: ¾" AB plywood, 10" x 36"
2. Sides of locker: ¾" AB plywood, 9¼" x 23¼" (two required)
3. Back of locker: ¾" AB plywood, 23¼" x 34½"
4. Bottom of locker: ¾" AB plywood, 8½" x 34½"
5. Shelf: ¾" AB plywood, 8½" x 34½"
6. Doors: ¾" AB plywood, 18" x 23¼" (two required)
7. Top of bench: 2" x 4" x 36" (six required)
8. Back of bench: 2" x 4" x 36"
9. Sides of bench: 2" x 4" x 21" (two required)
10. Front of bench: 2" x 4" x 36"
11. Legs: 2" x 4" x 26½" (four required)
12. Side braces: 2" x 4" x 21" (two required)
13. Back brace: 2" x 4" x 36"
14. Hinges: (four required)
15. Hasp: locking type
    Masonite top (optional) 24" x 36"
    Two tubes construction adhesive, 16d box nails (one pound), 6d
        finishing nails, eight 1½" flat head wood screws for mounting
        cabinet to bench top

Cut all materials as listed on the materials list. Assemble the top frame of the bench by attaching the front, back, and sides. Note that the two side pieces fit inside the front and back pieces. Use adhesive and 16d box nails. Nail the legs to the top frame, then nail the side and back braces. Nail the top 2x4s onto the top frame. Use construction adhesive for all joints and drive all nail heads below the surface with a nail set.

Build the cabinet. Use construction adhesive and 6d finishing nails to attach the sides, top, and bottom to the back. Mark the location of the internal shelf 12" up from the bottom. Apply a bead of adhesive along your marks, position the shelf, and nail through the outside and back of the cabinet. Mount the doors using the hinges and mounting screws. Finally, attach the locking hasp to the doors. Install the Masonite top at this time if desired. Mount the cabinet to the top of the reloading bench, screwing through the bottom of the cabinet into the 2x4 top.

The reloading bench can be painted or used as is. Put the bench in an area where you can work undisturbed. When not in use, keep all reloading supplies locked up.

SHADOWBOX FRAME

Use a shadowbox frame to display items such as trout and salmon flies, knives, an antique pistol, or any item that is relatively small and will decorate the wall in your den. A shadowbox frame is nothing more than a decorative picture frame over a box.

The required depth of the shadowbox will depend on what will be displayed. Fishing flies or lures require a box with a 1½" depth; knives require 3", and handguns need a depth of around 4". This plan is for a shadowbox for displaying trout flies.

Materials List

Frame:
> Sides, 1" x ⅝" x 8¾" (two required)
> Top and bottom, 1" x ⅝" x 12¾" (two required)

Box:
> Sides, ½" x 1½" x 8" (two required)
> Front and back, ½" x 1½" x 12" (two required)
> Back, ¼" x 12" x 8" Masonite or ¼" plywood

Glass:
> 7½" x 11½"

Wooden dowel (⅛" diameter) 1" long, as required

Green felt for lining interior of shadow box, 4d finishing nails, polyvinyl resin adhesive, hot melt glue, hanging hook, wood stain, clear finish.

Cut all materials according to the materials list. Make a dado cut (⅛" deep, ¼" wide) on the top, inside edge of the shadowbox pieces. This is where the glass is inset later. Build the box by miter cutting all ends (at 45 degrees) and assembling with finishing nails and adhesive. Then attach the back to the box.

Make a dado cut on the inside back of all frame pieces ⅜" wide and ¼" deep so that when the frame is assembled, it will fit down on the shadowbox. Miter cut the ends of the frame pieces and assemble the frame using adhesive and finishing nails.

At this point the glass should fit snugly into the top of the shadowbox and the frame should fit snugly over the top of the shadowbox.

Mark the location of the flies in the box. The photo shows a display of eleven evenly spaced flies, each about 2" from its neighbor. Drill ⅛" holes at these locations. Put a drop of adhesive on the tip of each dowel and insert in each hole.

After the adhesive has dried, apply stain and clear finish to all exterior pieces of the shadowbox frame and box. When dry, cover the inside surfaces of the shadowbox with green felt, making cuts for the dowels. Using hot glue, attach trout flies to the ends of the dowels. Use just a spot of hot glue and attach each fly at the bend of the hook. Keep a careful eye on alignment.

The final step is to install the glass and attach the frame to the shadowbox. Use adhesive and 4d finishing nails. Attach a hanging hook to the back top of the box and hang in a suitable spot.

RANGE BOX FOR HANDGUNS

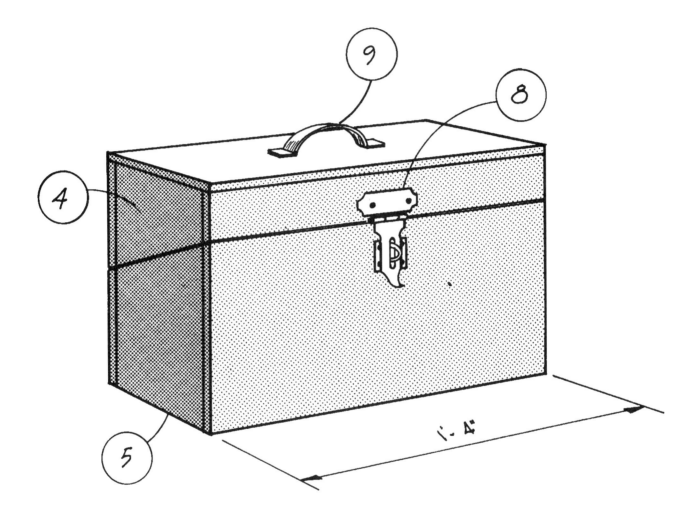

A range box is used to carry pistols, ammunition, hearing and eye protection equipment, and possibly a spotting scope to a shooting range. While these items can be carried in almost any type of case from an attachè case to a small suitcase, you will find the illustrated range box much more convenient to carry and use. Keep in mind, also, that many local ordinances require that pistols be carried in a case to and from a range. This project should meet those requirements.

Materials List

▼▼▼▼▼▼▼▼▼▼▼▼▼▼▼▼▼▼▼▼▼▼▼▼

All materials ½" AA plywood except as noted. One-half sheet required

1. Front: 16" x 8½"
2. Back: 16" x 8½"
3. Top: 16" x 9"
4. Ends: 8" x 8½" (two required)
5. Bottom: 15" x 8"
6. Insert: 5 x 8" (¾" pine)
7. Piano hinge: 16" long
8. Locking hasp
9. Carrying handle
   4d finishing nails, construction adhesive, wood stain, clear finish

▼▼

Cut the plywood as indicated in the materials list. Then cut the pistol insert as shown in the plan. Assemble the pieces to form a box using adhesive and 4d finishing nails. Do not install the pistol insert yet. Allow the adhesive to dry overnight. Next, mark a 2" line down from the top on one side of the box

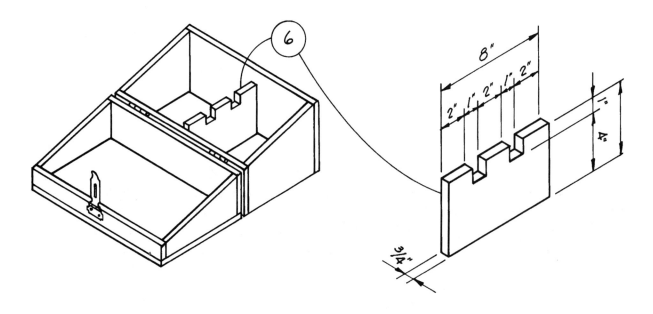

and 4½" up from the bottom on the opposite side. Draw a diagonal line on each end of the box which connects the line on the front and the line on the back. Using a hand-held circular saw or table saw, cut the box along these lines, forming two halves. Then install the pistol insert inside the box using adhesive and finishing nails.

Sand smooth all surfaces. Apply a coat of stain followed by two coats of clear finish, allowing each coat to dry before applying the next. When the finish has dried, apply felt strips to the pistol insert.

Fasten the piano hinge to the surface of the back, using wood screws. Attach the hasp to the face of the box, and install the handle to the top of the box. Now the range box is ready for the first of many trips to the range.

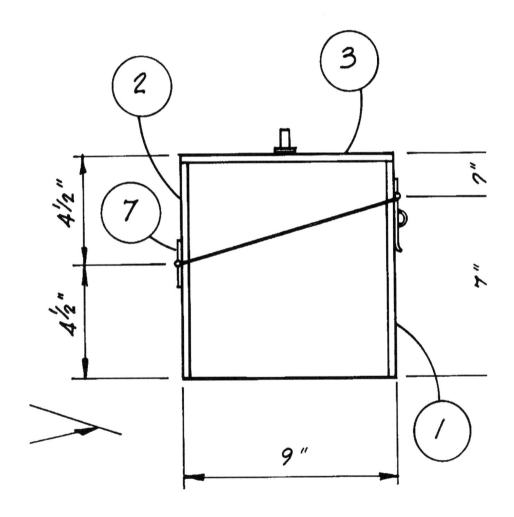

WOODEN BASE FOR SKEET THROWER ——————

The easiest way to practice shotgun shooting is at a trap and skeet range. If such a range is not close to your home, the next best way to practice is to use a mechanical trap that will throw clay pigeons for you to shoot at. A number of these units are on the market with prices ranging from about $50 to over $200. The less expensive units are not as stable as the more expensive models and, as a result, tend to jump as the spring-loaded arm throws the clay bird. The solution to this problem is to build a base for the thrower which will hold it steady.

Because there are several different types of clay bird traps, it is not possible to give specific instructions for building a base that will fit all throwers. It is possible, however, to give guidelines for all machines. Two types of bases can easily be built using plywood and dimensional lumber.

A plywood base for a clay bird trap should be roughly 4' x 4' and cut from ¾" plywood. Use CDX or marine plywood. Attach the thrower in the center of the plywood, using suitable size bolts, and the thrower will be ready for action. You may want to paint the plywood before mounting the thrower.

A skeet thrower mounted on a 4' x 4' piece of plywood cannot be moved or transported easily, unless you have a pickup truck.

The second type of base is made from two lengths of 2x4s. Build a wooden cross and mount the thrower to this with bolts going up through the 2x4s to the thrower. The advantage of this type is that the thrower can be taken off it for transporting in a small vehicle.

CANOE BOX

Canoe camping often results in wet equipment, especially when the route passes through sections of white water. Waterproof equipment bags are expensive and have a short life. They simply puncture easily and are then useless for keeping equipment dry. A good solution is to build a sturdy plywood box that is custom-fit for your canoe.

It is impossible to give dimensions for all canoes. This plan is for a 15' aluminum canoe. If your canoe is different, make adjustments to the basic plan.

Materials List
▼▼▼▼▼▼▼▼▼▼▼▼▼▼▼▼▼▼▼▼▼▼

Cut from one sheet ½" CDX plywood as follows:

Top and bottom: 24" x 24" (two required)
Sides: 12" x 23" (two required)
Front and back: 12" x 24" (two required)
One piano hinge: 24" long, two concealed handles, one hasp, eight 2"
    angle brackets, one tube of construction adhesive, 6d finishing nails,
    waterproof caulk, exterior primer, and paint.

▼▼▼

Cut all pieces of plywood as listed in the materials list. Then, using construction adhesive and finishing nails, attach the front and back to the bottom of the box. Add the sides using the same technique. Apply adhesive to all joints and use four or five nails for each joint. Attach the 2" angle brackets at all corner joints. Locate these 2" down from the top and 2" up from the bottom. The angle brackets will add strength to the box.

Apply a bead of waterproof caulking to all interior joints of the box. After the caulking has been applied, smooth it with a wet finger or the bowl of a spoon to force it into the joints.

Sand all surfaces, then apply a coat of exterior primer followed by two coats of paint to all surfaces. Allow sufficient drying time between coats. Light colors are best for summer use as the box will absorb less heat from sunlight.

Mount the top to the box using the piano hinge and mounting screws. Attach the hasp to the front of the box and the concealed handles to the sides.

Lash the canoe box into the canoe with nylon cord, tying the box to the cross members through the handles, to keep it in place and to keep the box in the canoe in the event of a dump in the river. While the contents of the box will become wet if the canoe flips, the box and contents will remain with the canoe.

FLOATING DOCK

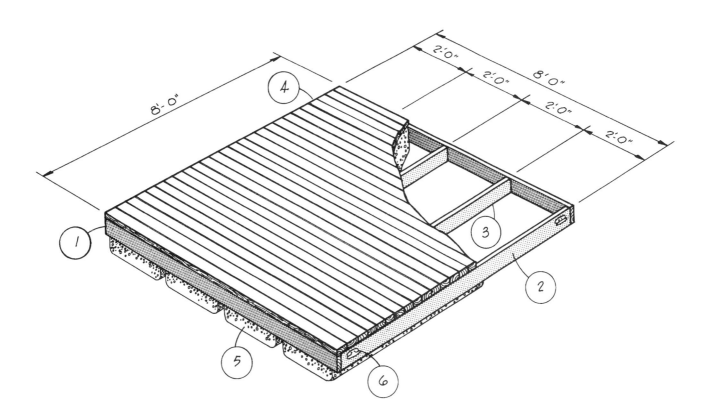

A floating dock or platform is something that you will want to consider if you have waterfront property. Local, state, or federal laws may require a permit to build or install such a dock. Before you begin this project, check with authorities—the Building Department or Wildlife Department, for examples—to see what local regulations require.

This floating dock platform is easy to build but not very easy to move on land. For this reason, build it close to the launching site. A front-end loader or backhoe can prove useful for moving it around. In the absence of heavy equipment, use large rollers such as lengths of 6" diameter fence posts.

Materials List

▼▼▼▼▼▼▼▼▼▼▼▼▼▼▼▼▼▼▼▼▼▼▼▼▼

All lumber is pressure-treated.

1. Sides: 2" x 6" x 8' (two required)
2. Front and back: 2" x 6" x 7' 9" (two required)
3. Braces: 2" x 6" x 7' 9" (three required)
4. Top: 2" x 4" x 8' (twenty-four required)
5. Closed-cell foam flotation batts: 2' x 8' x 10" (four required)
6. Cleats (four required)
   Anchor rope as required, four anchors, outdoor carpeting (64 square feet), 40' of 2' wide hardware cloth, two tubes panel adhesive, six tubes deck adhesive, twenty-five pounds of hot-dipped galvanized nails, 16d box type staple nails, and wire staples.

▼▼

Build the dock frame from 2x6 dimensional lumber with dividers spaced 2' apart. The dividers have a dual function. They add strength to the frame and offer a convenient way to attach the foam floatation batts, which are 2' wide.

It is common practice to cover the bottom of the frame with hardware cloth to hold the batts in place. Nail the top decking into place using adhesive and 16-penny galvanized nails. Space the decking ½" apart. Use a scrap of ½" plywood to get consistent spacing.

After the decking has been attached, flip the deck over and fit the batts in place. Some end trimming may be required. Four men can easily flip the deck. Loop the hardware cloth over the batts, nailing with staples into all of the cross members. The cloth is run perpendicular to the batts and is overlapped and tight. Trim the edges of cloth so that there are no sharp edges.

Once the frame has been built, the dock is launched. Four or more men can easily move the dock by hand using round fence posts and levers. If your area does not offer good terrain, consider hiring a backhoe or crane for moving it into the water.

After it has been launched, cover the top with outdoor carpeting. This will offer good footing when the dock gets wet. The pressure-treated lumber needs no finishing.

Tow the dock to the desired location and anchor. Use four weights, one at each corner, secured to the bottom of the dock.

In coastal areas, where tides rise and fall, the anchor lines should be long enough to hold the dock in place at high tide. This requires four anchors, four lighter weights, and four pulleys. Secure one end of each line to an anchor. Run the line through a pulley hanging under the dock. Tie the lighter weight to the end. The tide will lift the dock, and the weights will rise, but the dock will be anchored in place.

While all canoes have one or two seats, these tend to be uncomfortable and provide no back support. In truth, the main reason that a back supporting seat is not available is that the canoe—which has a tendency towards instability—would have a much higher center of gravity and be more inclined to tip over if a back supporting seat were available. This is also the reason that paddling is done from a kneeling position in the bottom of the canoe.

A back supporting seat can be made from plywood quite easily, and when used properly, will not raise the center of gravity the canoe.

This seat is not designed for use while paddling but rather as a back support when fishing. The user must sit in the bottom of the canoe to use this backrest.

Materials List

▼▼▼▼▼▼▼▼▼▼▼▼▼▼▼▼▼▼▼▼▼▼▼▼

¾" CDX plywood, 26" x 16", rounded top, no sharp edges

▼▼

The base of the seat must be cut to fit into the bottom of the canoe. Use a scrap piece of 1x2 lumber and a pencil to trace the bottom contour onto the canoe seat. First insert the seat into the canoe, perpendicular to the canoe bottom. Hold the pencil on top of the scrap lumber with the point of the pencil on the seat. Then move the block along the bottom of the canoe in front of the seat. This will transfer the contour of the canoe bottom onto the plywood.

Cut along this line with a saber saw. Check the fit of the cut piece in the canoe. Finish the seat with primer and paint or stain and clear finish.

The canoe seat is placed in front of an existing canoe seat strut and the user sits on the floor of the canoe. A boat cushion or life jacket can be placed in the bottom of the canoe for a more comfortable seat. The backrest is not fastened in place but relies on a close fit. The reason for this is so the seat can be easily removed when transporting the canoe or when negotiating difficult water.

PORTABLE DOG KENNEL

A portable dog kennel is a good way to transport your gun dog to a hunting area. Fiberglass kennels are required for shipping dogs on commercial aircraft and these are expensive. A functional and durable dog kennel can be easily constructed from plywood by the do-it-yourselfer. The project in this section can be used in the back of a pickup truck or most of the sport utility vehicles currently on the road.

The kennel project is for a medium size hunting dog, such as a springer or Brittany spaniel. Larger dogs, such as a Labrador retriever, will require more room. Add 2" to all piece sizes for a larger kennel.

Materials List

▼▼▼▼▼▼▼▼▼▼▼▼▼▼▼▼▼▼▼▼▼▼▼▼▼

All parts cut from 1½ sheets ½" CDX plywood

Top and bottom: 23" x 34" (two required)
Sides: 26" x 35" (two required)
Ends: 23" x 26" (two required)
One tube waterproof construction adhesive
One galvanized steel latch, bolt type
Two 2" galvanized butt hinges
One quart exterior primer
Two quarts exterior paint
One-half pound 6d finishing nails

▼▼

Cut all plywood pieces listed on the materials list. Since the kennel requires vent holes around the unit, begin cutting these with a saber saw, using the plunge cut. Vent holes are also handy for lifting and moving the kennel.

On each side panel cut two holes, each measuring 3" x 8" and located 4" down from the top edge. The back panel vent hole is the same dimension, centered and located 4" down from the top edge. The front panel has an identical vent hole, located 5" down from the top edge, and a door which measures 20" x 13". When tracing the door pattern, round the corners so there will be no sharp edges. Use a wood rasp, or similar tool, to round any sharp edges around the vent holes and door opening.

Begin assembly by attaching the side panels to the bottom. Use construction adhesive and finishing nails for all fastening. Next, attach the back panel, then the top. The front panel should be installed without the door at this time.

Allow the adhesive to set for several hours, then sand all surfaces. Next, apply a coat of exterior primer to all surfaces. Follow this with two coats of an exterior grade paint. Generally speaking, light colors are preferable to lessen the heating from the sun. Allow sufficient drying time between coats.

Once the paint has dried, attach the door by face-mounting the hinges along one side. Attach the latch on the opposite side of the door.

In use, place the kennel in the vehicle and jump the dog into the unit. A layer of hay or an old blanket in the bottom of the kennel will help to keep your hunting dog comfortable on a long drive.

PORTABLE HUNTING BLIND

**Portable hunting blind in position. Natural materials need
to be woven between poultry netting.**

A portable hunting blind is an excellent way for duck and goose hunters to conceal themselves during the hunt. While a number of commercially made portable hunting blinds are available, they all fall far short of doing a good job of concealment because they are not made from native materials. To be truly effective, a portable hunting blind should blend in with the surrounding landscape and plants.

The only way a hunting blind can blend in with the surroundings is to use grasses, reeds, beach debris, and other materials from the immediate area as part of the blind. Any other blind materials will stand out from the landscape and indicate danger to waterfowl.

The project in this section will offer concealment for two adult hunters. The basic frame can be built in the workshop, then transported to the hunting area for finishing with natural native materials.

Materials List

▼▼▼▼▼▼▼▼▼▼▼▼▼▼▼▼▼▼▼▼▼▼▼▼

8' of 2" wide mesh poultry netting, 3' high
Four 2" x 2" x 3' lumber
Two 2" x 2" x 5' lumber
Two 5" stove bolts with wing nuts and two washers
One can spray paint, flat olive drab
⁹⁄₁₆" staples

▼▼

Drill a ⅜" hole, 2" down from one end of each of the 5' long 2x2 lumber. Next drill a ⅜" hole, 2" down from one end of two of the 3' long 2x2 lumber.

Spray paint all surfaces of the 2x2 lumber.

Lay the four 3' long 2x2 pieces side by side on a flat surface so that the distance between the first and last piece equals 8'. The two end pieces should have ⅜" holes, 2" down from the top.

Staple the poultry netting to the 3' long lumber. Drive at least eight staples into each piece to securely hold the netting to the lumber. Flip the blind over and attach one 5' long piece of 2x2 lumber with a stove bolt to the top of one side of the blind. Do the same for the other side. Stand the blind up and tighten the wing nuts to hold the blind in an upright position.

In use, the blind is carried to the hunting area and set up. The face of the blind should be curved into a half-moon shape. Then the blind must be concealed by weaving materials from the area into the face of the poultry netting. Place additional native materials around the sides of the blind.

CHAPTER 4
BACKYARD & GARDEN PROJECTS
▼▼▼

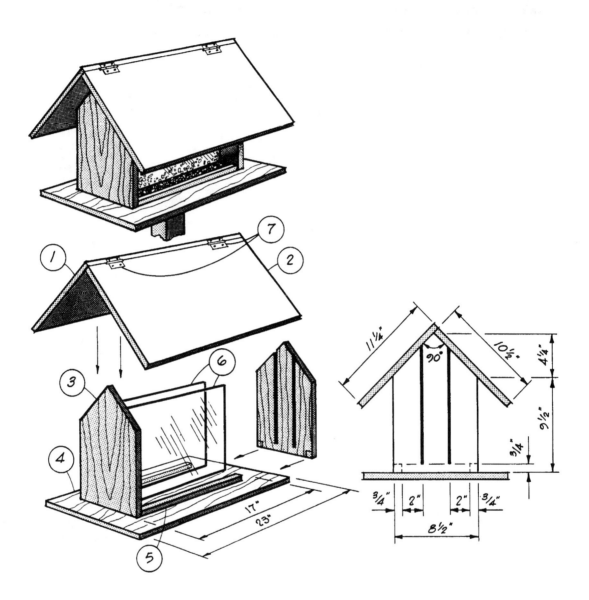

A bird feeder in the yard will attract wild birds during the winter. Wild birds often find it difficult to find food during this time and will flock to a well-stocked feeder all season. Once you feed wild birds, they become dependent on you for food and you must keep the feeder full at all times.

The food you put out will depend on the birds in your area. A wild bird seed mixture is best for many birds. It is widely available in supermarkets, home improvement centers, and feed stores. In all probability, the mixture you buy will be right for the birds in your area.

Commercially made bird feeders range in price from $10 to $50. A do-it-yourselfer with minimum woodworking skills can quickly make an attractive and functional feeder. While a bird feeder can be as simple as a board nailed to a windowsill, the project in this section is much more versatile and should last for many seasons with no care other than filling with seeds.

Materials List
▼▼▼▼▼▼▼▼▼▼▼▼▼▼▼▼▼▼▼▼▼▼▼▼▼

1. Top: 1" redwood, 11¼" x 24"
2. Top: 1" redwood, 10½" x 24"
3. Ends: 1" redwood, 8½" x 13¾" (two required, cut as indicated)
4. Base: ¾" CDX plywood, 15" x 23"
5. Parting strip: pine, ¾" x ¾" x 15" (two required)
6. Dividers: ¼" Plexiglas, 10" x 15½" (two required)
7. Hinges: galvanized, 2" long, (two required)
   Galvanized steel L brackets 2" long (two required for mounting feeder to post)
   Adhesive
   Galvanized 4d finishing nails
   Paint if desired
   Post for mounting: 4" x 4", 7' long
   Concrete

▼▼

Cut the pieces of redwood and plywood as indicated in the materials list. Cut the end panels as shown in the plan. Make two ¼" x ¼" dado cuts on each of the end pieces to receive the Plexiglas dividers. The dado cuts can be made on a table saw or with a hand-held router. The cuts must stop ½" up from the bottom and be located 2¾" in from each side.

Begin assembly by attaching the parting strips to the base. These are located as indicated in the illustration. Attach the end pieces to the base, and insert the Plexiglas into the dado cuts in the end pieces. Nail the larger top section (#1) over the end pieces. Note that this top section should extend ¾" over the top of the end pieces so that the other top section (#2) will be flush when installed. Attach the second top section with hinges to the first top section. During construction—with the exception of the second top section—use waterproof adhesive and galvanized finishing nails. Finish with paint or clear finish if desired.

The bird feeder should be mounted on a post in the yard. Dig a post hole at least 2' deep. Then place the 7' long 4x4 post into the hole. Add concrete to hold the post steady and plumb up the post with the aid of a 4' level. Use scrap lumber to hold the post in position until the concrete sets. Allow the concrete to harden at least overnight, then attach the feeder with galvanized L brackets to the top of the post. Now all that is required is to keep the feeder full during the season and enjoy the variety of wild birds that will come for food.

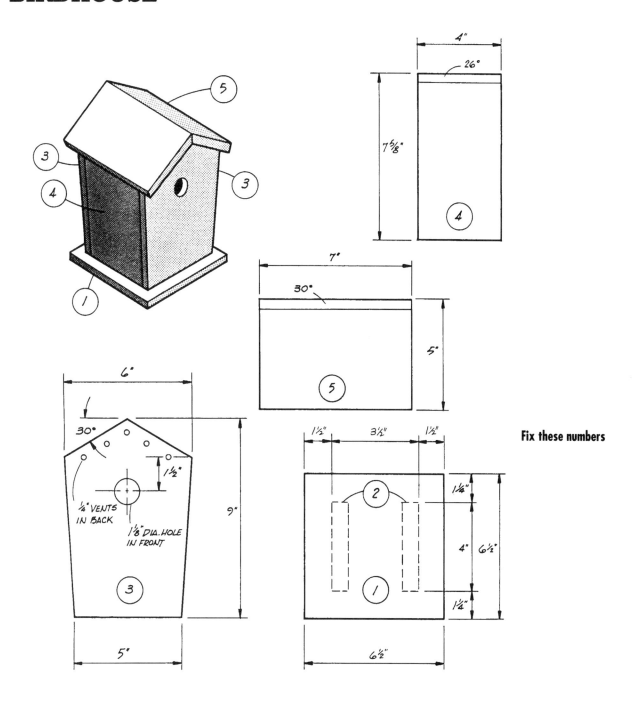

Fix these numbers

Building a birdhouse is easier than attracting nesting birds. Poor design, the wrong size entry hole, location of the house, and a score of other things can result in a birdhouse that is of little interest to the birds in your area. For this reason, the birdhouse illustrated in this section should be built exactly as shown. This birdhouse is for small birds such as chickadees, tufted titmice, wrens, and nuthatches.

Materials List

▼▼▼▼▼▼▼▼▼▼▼▼▼▼▼▼▼▼▼▼▼▼▼▼▼

All parts are cut from 1" x 8" clear heart redwood

1. Base: 6½" x 6½"
2. Cleats: 1" x ¾" x 4" (two required)
3. Front and back: 9" x 6", cut as indicated
4. Sides: 4" x 7⅝" (two required)
5. Roof: 5" x 7" (two required)

▼▼

Cut the pieces as indicated in the materials list. Note that the front and back pieces (#3) are 6" wide at the top and 5" wide at the bottom and that the tops of these pieces are cut at a 30° angle. The back piece has five ¼" vent holes along the top edges, and the entry hole (1⅛" in diameter) is 3" down from the top on the front piece.

In addition, the two side pieces (#4) have a bevel top edge, cut at a 26° angle. The two roof sections (#5) also are bevel cut at a 30° angle so that when assembled they will mate for a tight fit.

Once all of the pieces have been cut and the edges beveled correctly, assemble by attaching the cleats (#2) to the base, the front and back to the ends of the cleats, and the sides to the cleats, front, and back. Finally, attach the two top sections. Use a waterproof adhesive and 6d, galvanized finishing nails.

The birdhouse can be painted, but because it is made from clear heart redwood, it will look good for a long time if coated with linseed oil and allowed to weather. Put the finished birdhouse in a sheltered area so that it will be out of harsh weather and high enough so that predators such as cats will not be a problem. Use an eyebolt, placed in the center of the roof ridge, and nylon cord for hanging from a tree limb.

PATIO DECK

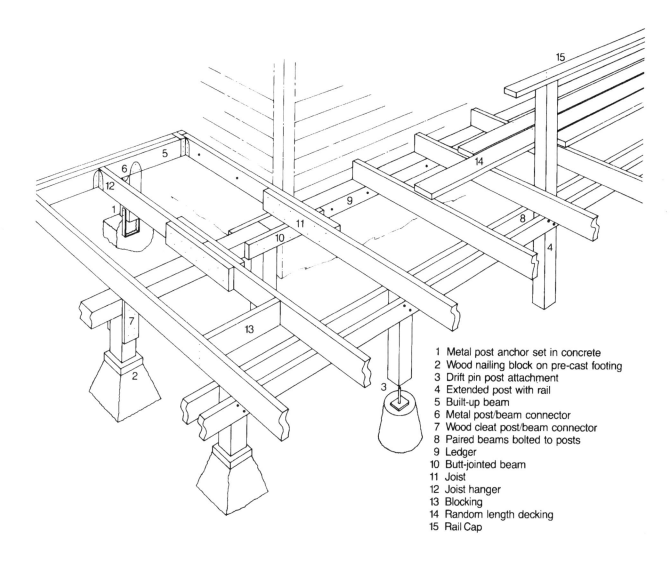

1 Metal post anchor set in concrete
2 Wood nailing block on pre-cast footing
3 Drift pin post attachment
4 Extended post with rail
5 Built-up beam
6 Metal post/beam connector
7 Wood cleat post/beam connector
8 Paired beams bolted to posts
9 Ledger
10 Butt-jointed beam
11 Joist
12 Joist hanger
13 Blocking
14 Random length decking
15 Rail Cap

Detail of wooden deck - Courtesy, California Redwood Association

A wooden patio deck will quickly become a favorite place for relaxing or entertaining family and friends. In addition, many real estate experts say that a wooden deck will increase the value of your home by a figure that is almost double the cost of the materials used to construct the deck.

Wooden decks can be made from redwood or pressure-treated lumber. Redwood is beautiful to look at and weathers well over time. Unfortunately, the farther you live from the redwood forests of northern California and the

Pacific Northwest, the higher the price for this lumber. Do-it-yourselfers on the East Coast, for example, will quickly learn that a wooden deck made from pressure-treated lumber will cost about half as much as the same size deck made from redwood. If cost is a factor, chances are good that you will want to build with pressure-treated lumber rather than redwood. Standard building practices are the same for both types of lumber.

While it is not possible to give specific plans for building a wooden deck for your home, it will be helpful to give guidelines for building a variety of decks. Then you will be able to plan your own deck based on your personal needs, grade, and local building codes. Most decks are composed of the basic parts shown in the diagram.

FOOTINGS

Deck footings rest on the ground and support the deck posts or uprights. Footings may either be concrete blocks, precast pier blocks, or poured concrete pads. As a rule of thumb, a footing should be about twice the size of the post it supports. For example, 4x4 posts should rest on 8" x 8" concrete footings.

Building codes are usually specific about the form and placement of footings. In general, they are required to extend below the frost line and they should extend above the ground to keep wooden posts away from ground moisture.

Mixing and pouring concrete footings is a simple, though laborious job. Cement, sand, gravel, and water mixed in a wheelbarrow can be poured into a mold without much difficulty. Premixed (dry) cement is generally available and all that need be added is the proper amount of water. Molds or forms can be built from scrap lumber. Forms, such as Sona Tubes, can be purchased from building supply stores.

Placement of the footings is key to the deck's stability. The number of footings and posts needed depends on the size of beams. In general, builders use heavier beams to minimize the number of footings required. The placement of footings can be calculated from the suggested beam and joist spans.

POSTS

Posts, sometimes called uprights, are vertical members which rest on the footings and support the beams and joists. The length of the posts is critical in establishing the height of the deck. Plan ahead—extended posts can serve as a support for railings, benches, and trellises.

Timbers which measure 4" x 4" and larger are most often used for posts. If large crowds, deep snow, or other heavy loads are anticipated, or if the deck is elevated, larger posts may be needed and cross bracing may be necessary to prevent lateral movement. Your local building department, which establishes building codes, and home improvement centers are good sources of information about post sizes for the deck you are planning.

Beams can rest on top of posts, or double beams can straddle the post. The double beam method uses two pieces of thinner dimensional lumber. Sometimes this can mean a savings. If the double-beam method is used, the posts need to be larger.

If a single beam will rest on top of the post, the post top must be trimmed squarely to make a solid seat for the beam. Double-check measurements before cutting. Measure and level the post from a stable reference point. Make sure all posts are plumb when they are installed.

DECKING

Most decks consist of 2x4 or 2x6 lumber, face-nailed to the joists. Some builders prefer to use decking screws. In either case, countersink the nail or screw heads. Use only hot-dipped galvanized nails or decking screws to prevent unsightly staining of the wood.

▼▼▼▼▼▼▼▼▼▼▼▼▼▼▼▼▼▼▼▼▼▼

Use a level to check plumb of joists - Courtesy, California Redwood Association

▲▲▲▲▲▲▲▲▲▲▲▲▲▲▲▲▲▲▲▲▲▲▲▲

When nailing or screwing, place two fasteners per location. Nail in either a straight or zig-zag pattern, but be consistent. Avoid over driving nails with the hammer or you will cause "moon" shapes on the deck which will collect dirt and water.

Use full length lumber where possible to minimize butt joints on the deck surface. Planning is the key here. If your plan calls for a deck which measures 8' wide by 10' long, run the decking lengthwise and purchase 10' decking material. This makes for a more attractive deck.

When using redwood for decking, the top of the deck can be left to weather naturally or coated with boiled linseed oil to bring out the natural beauty of the redwood. Pressure-treated lumber does not need a finish coating although some finishes make a pressure-treated deck look nicer.

STAIRS

If the deck is more than a foot off the ground, you should build stairs. Stairs require precision carpentry and quality materials. Decay resistance is important, so an all-heartwood redwood or pressure-treated lumber should be used.

Stairs for a deck are made with treads and stringers. The treads are the stepping surface and are supported by the stringers. Stair treads should be a minimum of 11" wide and between 6" and 7" apart. For wide stairs, stringers, which have been notched for the treads and placed 24" apart will provide enough support. When two steps are planned, a 2x12 can be laid on edge or notched as a stringer. If more steps are needed, a sloping stringer should be used. Building codes commonly require that notched stringers have a minimum of 3½" of width below the notch.

As an alternative, stair treads can be set inside a pair of stringers, so that the stringers enclose them on both sides. These are called boxed stringers. The tread can then be supported by cleats nailed to the stringers or by separate notched stringers. Space stringers 24" on center to provide ample support for the treads.

At the top, anchor the stringers to the deck framing. At the bottom, anchor them to the deck at the next lower level or rest them on a concrete pad or footings.

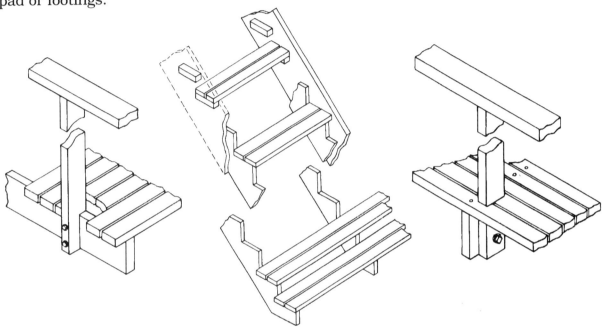

Stair and Railing detail - Courtesy, California Redwood Association

RAILINGS

Although the railings are often the last of the finishing touches, they need to be planned in advance. Railings are necessary for any deck over 1½' off the ground. In many areas a railing is required by code for any deck.

Design a railing that doesn't encourage sitting unless it is built for that purpose. Lengths of 2x2 lumber, centered and nailed to the top of the railing is one method often used to discourage rail sitting. Another method is to build the railing to a height that is not convenient for sitting—5' high, for example. Railings should be sturdy barriers erected at the deck's edge without obscuring the view.

Railing supports should be securely fastened to the framing of the deck. Toenailing to the surface is almost never adequate. Railing supports should be bolted to joists or beams, or they may be an extension of the posts.

Vertical grain redwood or pressure-treated lumber is suggested for the cap of a deck rail because they best resist weathering and splintering.

DOG KENNEL

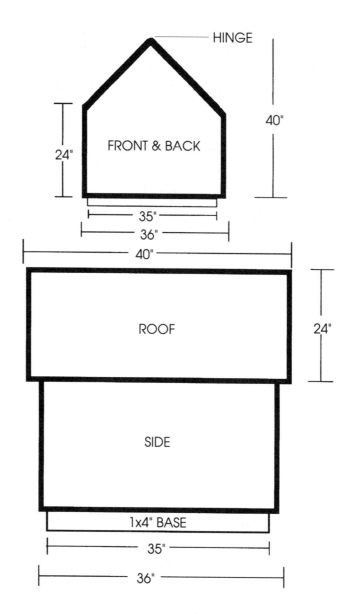

HINGE

FRONT & BACK

24"

40"

35"

36"

40"

ROOF

24"

SIDE

1x4" BASE

35"

36"

If you keep your dog outdoors all of the time, or during the day when you are away, you should have a place for him to get out of the weather. A kennel will protect your dog from the elements and probably prevent the early onset of old age in the animal. A kennel need not be elaborate, but there are some guidelines that should be followed for the house to be effective.

Build the kennel to fit your dog snugly. Such a kennel should be large enough for the dog to curl up in and retain his natural body heat. Medium-size dogs need about 30" x 30". For larger dogs add about 6" per side; smaller dogs, subtract 6" per side.

The kennel should be raised off the ground to help insulate the house from the moisture and cold in the ground. The bottom edges of the kennel should be sealed to prevent drafts. A flap of canvas, weighted along the bottom and wider than the width of the opening, makes for an easy entry and will also help to keep out drafts.

The sidewalls and roof should be sealed to prevent heat loss and prevent drafts. The roof should be hinged along the top to permit changes of bedding every few months. If you live in an area where the winters are bitter cold, consider a double-walled kennel built along the same principles as your home. Space the walls ¾" to 1" apart and fill the space with cellulose insulation before attaching the roof. Additionally, you can cover the interior of the roof with foil-faced foam insulation.

Materials List
▼▼▼▼▼▼▼▼▼▼▼▼▼▼▼▼▼▼▼▼▼▼▼

All parts ½" CDX plywood except as noted (two sheets required)

Roof: 24" x 40" (two required)
Sides: 24" x 36" (two required)
Front and back: 36" x 40" (two required)
Floor: 35" x 35"
Base: 1" x 4" x 34" (five required), one piece 1" x 4" x 33"
Draft Board: 1" x 4" x 35"
Piano hinge (40" long)
Waterproof adhesive, exterior primer and paint, roll roofing, 6d box nails, canvas for door cover

▼▼▼

Cut all parts from two sheets of plywood, making door opening 18" high. Make a frame from the 1x4 lumber with a center strut to add strength. Nail the floor to this frame. Attach the sidewalls, front, and back to the base, using plenty of adhesive and at least four nails per joint. Install draft board on inside of doorway. Hang weighted canvas door over doorway. Nail on one side of the roof. Attach the second roof piece with the piano hinge. Cover roof with roll roofing. Apply primer and two coats of exterior paint, allowing sufficient drying time between coats.

Locate kennel so that doorway does not face into prevailing winds.

POTTING BENCH

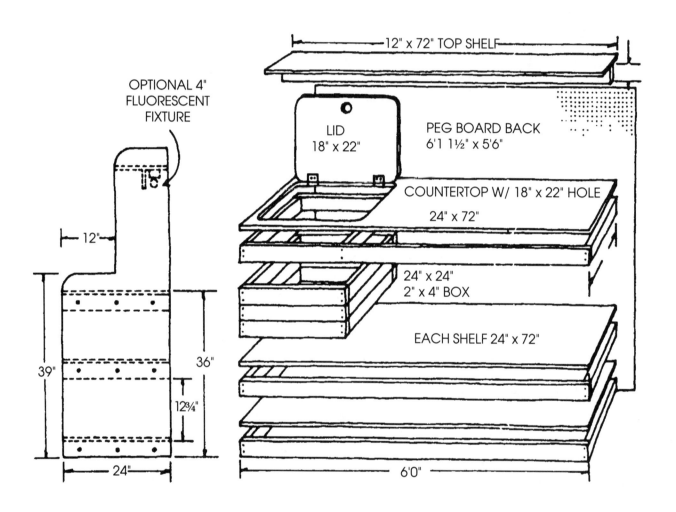

OPTIONAL 4"
FLUORESCENT
FIXTURE

12"

39"

36"

12¾"

24"

12" x 72" TOP SHELF

LID
18" x 22"

PEG BOARD BACK
6'1 1½" x 5'6"

COUNTERTOP W/ 18" x 22" HOLE
24" x 72"

24" x 24"
2" x 4" BOX

EACH SHELF 24" x 72"

6'0"

This is an ideal plywood project if someone in your family does a lot of gardening. The unit is compact yet versatile and will look good indoors or out close to the garden. A soil bin and lots of counter space make potting plants, transplanting, and planting seeds an enjoyable task. This is an ideal working place for a variety of garden-related chores.

Materials List

▼▼▼▼▼▼▼▼▼▼▼▼▼▼▼▼▼▼▼▼▼▼▼▼

Three sheets: ¾" exterior, A-B grade plywood
One and one-half sheets: ¼" thick pegboard (4' x 8')
2x4s, 6' long (six required)
2x4s, 21" long (six required)
2x4s, 24" long for soil bin front (six required)
2x4s, 21" long for soil bin sides (six required)
2' x 6' piece of plastic laminate (optional)
4' long fluorescent light fixture (optional)
2" butt hinges (six required)
Waterproof adhesive
Five pounds #8 galvanized finishing nails
Eighteen #10 roundhead wood screws
Exterior primer and paint

▼▼

Cut all 2x4s to the lengths given in the materials list. Build three 2' x 6' frames with the first two listed. Cut three ¾" plywood shelves, 2' x 6'. Note that the top shelf has an 18" x 22" cut-out for the soil bin. Mark this location carefully and cut with a saber saw. Drill a 1" hole in the cut-out as a finger pull for opening. Save the cut-out. This is the lid for the soil bin. Attach the plywood to the frames.

To make the soil bin, use six pieces of 2x4, cut as listed. Use adhesive and nails to construct three box frames, each 24" x 24".

Shape the two side panels from two 72" x 24" pieces of plywood as shown in the illustration. Drill screw holes and attach the sides of the bench to the shelves. Using screws, attach the bottom shelf first, then the middle and top shelves. Note that the three soil bin frames are located under the lid, between the middle and top shelf. Use waterproof adhesive for joining the soil bin sections. (To make the soil bin transportable for filling, nail a 2' x 2' piece of exterior plywood to the bottom of the bin.)

Nail a scrap of 2x4 lumber as a stop for the lid under the front edge of the soil bin cut-out. Attach the pegboard back pieces. If you are including a plastic laminate top, cover the bench top first and make the cut-out for the soil bin. Cover the soil bin lid with laminate and trim. Attach the lid to the counter top with the hinges.

To install a light fixture, attach it to the top shelf behind the 1x4 lumber. Install the top shelf using adhesive and screws.

Apply a coat of exterior primer to all surfaces. Follow with two coats of exterior paint, allowing ample drying time between coats. After the paint is dry, line the soil bin with plastic sheeting and fill with soil.

GARDEN TOOL STORAGE SHED ————————

While working in the home garden is supposed to be light labor, we all accumulate a wide variety of tools to help us. In addition to a mower, tiller, spreader, wheelbarrow, string trimmer, and leaf blower, most homes usually have rakes, shovels, hoes, hoses, and other useful tools. Add to this seeds, fertilizers, and weed killers, and equipment for applying them, and you can easily fill up the family garage quickly. The best solution is to have a place just for these items. The project in this section is just that.

The garden tool storage shed contains thirty-two square feet of usable space and it will fit easily into almost any yard. In addition, this shed can also be used for poolside storage of both garden and pool-related items. The wide doors make it easy to get tools and equipment in or out. Inside, you can add shelves and hooks for hanging and storing smaller tools and bicycles.

The shed is constructed from ⅜" APA grade-trademarked rough sawn plywood. The unit measures 6' 8" high in front and 4' 6" high at the back. A bed of gravel and a redwood or treated lumber sill make it resistant to deterioration from ground water. Steel pike stakes, bolted to the frame, secure the shed firmly in place. These can be just as easily unbolted for relocation.

Materials List
▼▼▼▼▼▼▼▼▼▼▼▼▼▼▼▼▼▼▼▼▼▼▼▼▼▼▼▼▼

Six 4' x 8' sheets of ⅜" rough-sawn plywood siding
Seventeen 2" x 2" x 8' lumber
Four 2" x 3" x 8' redwood or pressure treated lumber
Five 2" x 4" x 8' lumber
Four ¾" x 12" steel pipe for anchor posts
Fourteen ⁵⁄₁₆" carriage bolts with wing nuts, 4" long for sides
Four ⁵⁄₁₆" carriage bolts with wind nuts, 3" long
Twenty ⁵⁄₁₆" long carriage bolts with wing nuts, 2½" long
Four door hinges
Silicone caulk for all joints
Waterproof adhesive
Exterior primer and paint
Roll roofing to cover 40 sq. ft.
Gravel (as required for layer 4" deep under shed)
1x4 lumber for exterior trim (optional).

This shed is constructed by building sections then joining them.
Cut framing materials as follows and assemble according to diagram:

Bottom sills, front and back - 2 pieces 2x4 - 7' 8¼" redwood

Side sills - 2 pieces 2x4 - 4' long redwood (one per side)

Side framing (left and right)
    Two pieces: 2x2 - 4' long at rear
    Two pieces: 2x2 - 5'5" long at center
    Two pieces: 2x2 - 6'5" long at front
    Two pieces: 2x2 - 4'9" long at top
    Bottom pieces are listed as side sills

Back Framing
    Three pieces: 2x2 - 4' long at sides and center
    Two pieces: 2x2 - 3' 1½" long, intermediate verticals
    One piece: 2x2 - 7' 8¼" long, top horizontal
    Two pieces: 2x2 - 3' 7⅞" long for intermediate horizontal
    Bottom piece listed as bottom sill

Front Framing

Two pieces: 2x2 - 6' 1½" long at sides
One piece: 2x2 - 7' 8¼" long, top horizontal
One piece: 2x2 - 8" long, vertical at joint above door
One piece: 2x4 - 7' 5¼" long, header above door
Two pieces: 2x2 - 5' 1½" long, hinge strips
Bottom piece is listed as bottom sill

Doors

Four pieces: 2x2 - 5' long at sides
Two pieces: 2x2 - 3' long at top
Two pieces: 2x2 - 2' 9" long at bottom
Two pieces: 2x4 - 2' 9" long, tool hangers

Roof

Three pieces: 2x4 - 4' 6" long, roof joists
Two pieces: 2x4 - 7' 8¼" long, front and back, rip to fit

▼▼

Cut the plywood according to the diagram. Place panels face down when using a hand-held circular saw and face up when using a table saw. Measure and mark all cuts carefully. Use a chalk line to mark long cuts.

Assemble the parts, left side, right side, front and back, by attaching the 2x2 lumber to the backsides of the panels. Carefully check the diagram, to determine the location of the 2x2 lumber. Use adhesive and 6d galvanized nails to fasten the pieces.

After all parts have been constructed, begin bolting the parts together to form the building. This assembly should be done where the shed will be located. Four inches of gravel should be spread over the area before starting.

Bolt the left side to the back piece. Next, attach the right side to the back. Then bolt the front to the sides in the same manner. Carefully align the pieces and drill bolt holes through the 2x2 lumber. Apply a coat of adhesive to mating surfaces and tighten the bolts.

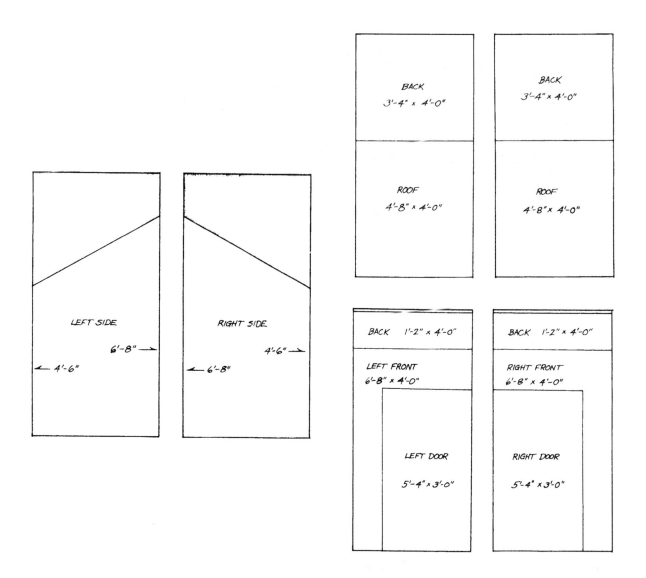

Garden tool storage shed - panel cutting layout

Once the shell of the building has been constructed, nail the roof sheeting to the rafters. Attach the roll roofing according to package directions. Drive steel pike stakes into ground, inside the shed, then bolt through sill plate to secure the building. Assemble the doors by fastening the 2x2 lumber to the backside of each panel. Note the placement of the 2x2 lumber in the diagram. Install the doors in the front of the building using hinges. Attach 1x4 lumber for an exterior trim, if desired. Next, caulk all joints. Apply one coat of exterior primer to all surfaces followed by two coats of paint. Allow sufficient drying time between coats.

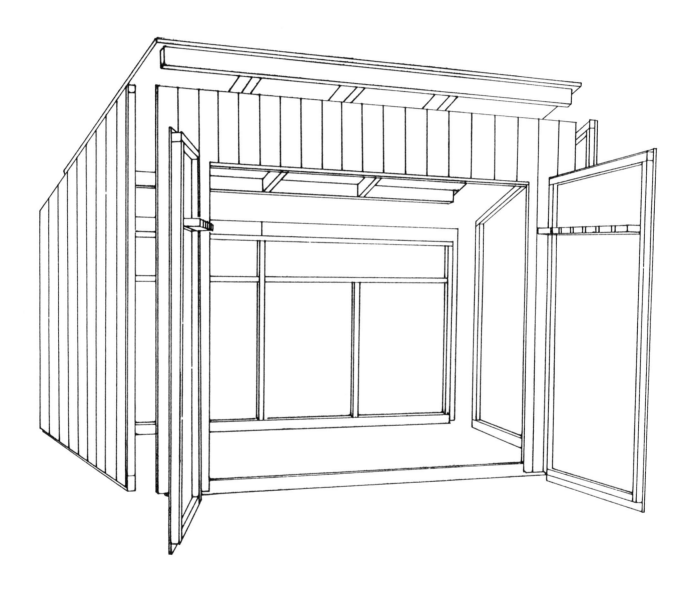

Garden tool storage shed - Exploded View

Picnic table - Courtesy American Plywood Association

A picnic table is a wonderful place to share an outdoor meal with family and friends during the summer. A commercially made picnic table can easily cost over $100 and usually requires assembly. The picnic table project in this section is easy to build, even for a beginning woodworker, and costs just a fraction of what a store-bought picnic table sells for. In addition, it will seat four adults or six children with ease. When finished with primer and paint, this picnic table will provide a comfortable place to spend time outdoors for many seasons. It is also lightweight so it can easily be moved into storage during the off season.

Materials List
▼▼▼▼▼▼▼▼▼▼▼▼▼▼▼▼▼▼▼▼▼▼

¾" AC exterior plywood (one sheet required)
3" x 5" angle braces with screws (six required)
3" x 3" angle braces with screws (four required)
Waterproof adhesive
6d galvanized finishing nails
Wood filler paste
Exterior primer and paint.

▼▼

Mark the pattern on the sheet of plywood as indicated in the panel layout diagram. With the aid of a table saw and a friend or using a hand-held circular saw, cut the panel width-wise at the 42" mark. Now the panel can be handled by one person much easier. Make the cuts for table top and the seat crosspieces on a table saw or with a hand-held circular saw. Cut the seats, sides, and supports with a saber or bayonet saw. Use a blade that is designed for cutting plywood. The shaded areas on the diagram indicate waste material. Know in advance that all cuts will result in pieces that are slightly smaller than the diagram, roughly the width of the saw blade.

Begin assembly. Attach each seat crosspiece to a seat using two of the smaller angle braces and screws. In addition, use waterproof adhesive and finishing nails (driven down through the seat top) for joining the crosspiece to the seat.

Attach the table support braces to the sides of the table. Adhesive and finishing nails should be used for greater strength. Attach the seats in position. Note in the diagram the location of the longer angle braces attached to the sides and under the seats. Attach the table top. Use adhesive and finishing nails (driven down through the top) to add strength to the table.

After the table has been assembled and the adhesive has dried, countersink and fill all nail holes with the paste filler material. Once this material has dried hard, sand flush with the surface. Sand the entire picnic table, paying close attention to the top of the table and seats. In addition, the table top and seat corners should be rounded and smooth, leaving no sharp edges to catch clothing.

Once the picnic table has been sanded smooth, dust and apply a coat of primer. Follow this with two coats of exterior paint, allowing drying time between coats.

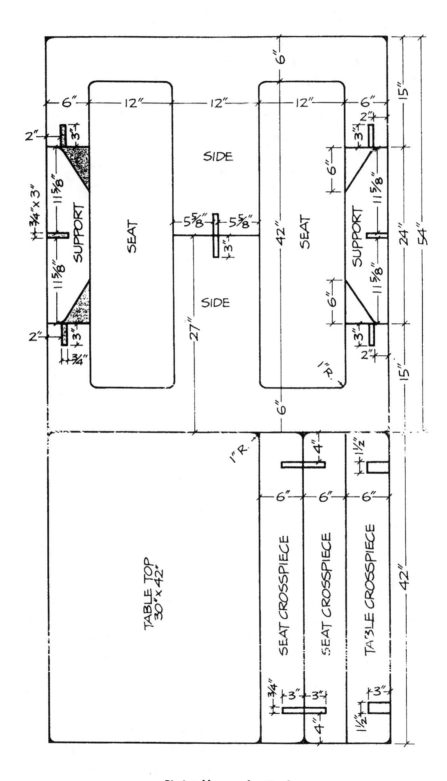

Picnic table - panel cutting layout

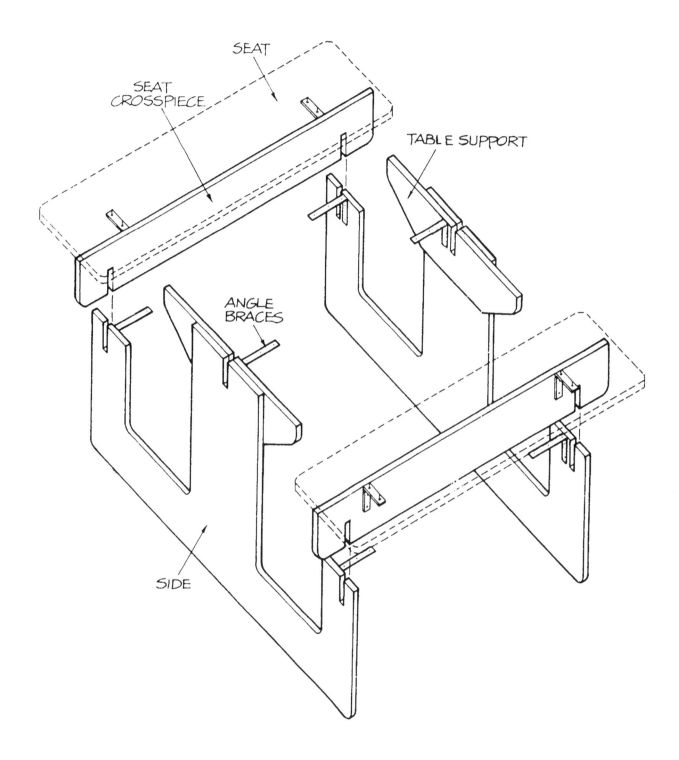

SEAT

SEAT
CROSSPIECE

TABLE SUPPORT

ANGLE
BRACES

SIDE

Picnic table - Exploded View

WOODEN PLANTER BOX

Redwood planter boxes - Courtesy, California Redwood Association

This plan for a handsome planter is courtesy of the California Redwood Association and well worth building. Because it is made with a base of construction heart redwood, it can be placed on soil without fear of the wood rotting over time. As you can see from the photograph, it also looks great on a redwood deck.

Materials List

▼▼▼▼▼▼▼▼▼▼▼▼▼▼▼▼▼▼▼▼▼▼▼▼▼▼

Construction heart redwood:
  Four: 4" x 4" x 15" pieces
  Sixteen: 1" x 4" x 22½" pieces
  Four: 2" x 6" x 22½" pieces
  Two: 2" x 4" x 24½" pieces
Construction common redwood:
  Sixteen: 1" x 4" x 22½" pieces
  Eight: 2" x 2" x 15" pieces
  Four: 1" x 4" x 26½" pieces
Nails:
  Sixty 12-penny, galvanized
  One hundred-sixty 6-penny, galvanized

▼▼▼

Nail two 2x2s to adjacent faces of each 4x4 corner post. Use 12d nails and be sure to leave ¾" for the 1x4 panels to fit flush with the outer faces of the 4x4 posts. Next, attach the 1x4 boards to posts using two 6d nails at each board end. The 1x4 boards should be evenly spaced along the post and flush with the bottom, top, and outer face. Use construction heart 1x4s for interior walls and construction common for exterior walls.

Complete two walls, both inside and out, to form an L as shown in the illustration. Then construct the last two walls, completing the box. It may help to lay the project on its side when nailing the last walls.

For the base, on the bottom of the box place two 2x4s on opposite sides, 1" in from the edge. Nail the 2x4s to the 4x4 posts with two 12d nails in each end of the boards. Drill two 1-inch drainage holes in two of the 2x6s to be used for the bottom of the planter.

For the top, butt-join 1x4s flush with the planter's edge. Use two 6d nails at each board end, penetrating the 4x4 at one end and the 2x2 at the other. These nails can be countersunk and filled with a non-oily filler paste material.

Interior surfaces should be lined with a polyethylene liner. Provide drainage by cutting holes through the bottom of the planter and the liner.

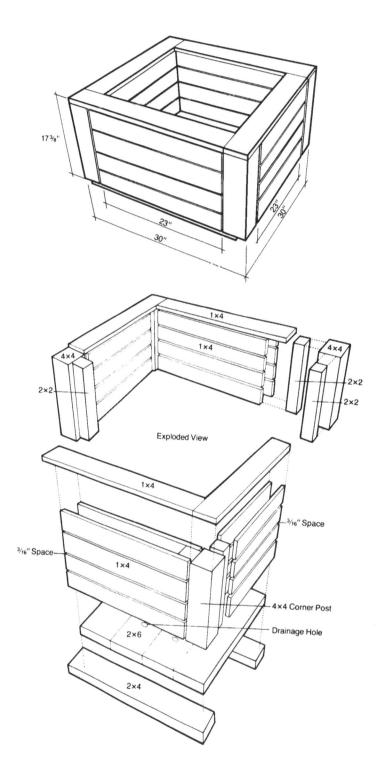

Redwood planter box - detail - Courtesy, California Redwood Association

RAISED-BED GARDEN

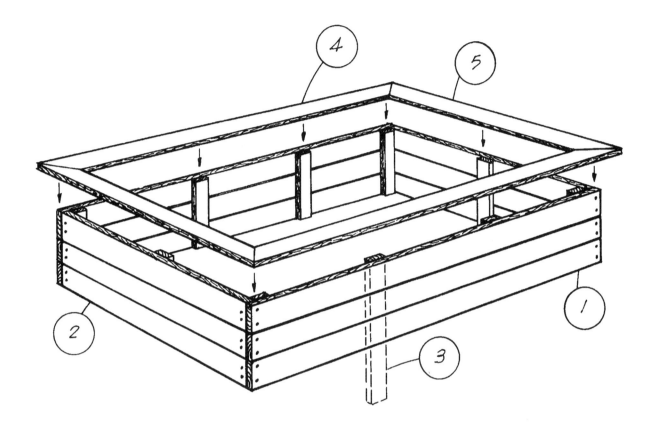

Raised-bed gardens are an excellent choice for the urban gardener with a small amount of space or for any gardener with poor soil conditions. Raised-bed garden frames can be built from timbers, pressure-treated lumber, or redwood and filled with a good grade topsoil, compost, and peat moss for an ideal growing medium.

Raised-bed gardens generally drain well and are easier to work because they are raised above the ground. This makes them an ideal choice for handicapped or elderly gardeners who find tending a conventional garden difficult. Lastly, vegetables and flowers can be planted closer together in a raised bed garden, thus the yield is commonly greater than in a conventional garden.

Raised-bed gardens can be simple or complex but you must follow some basic construction guidelines or the structure will bulge or burst apart at the seams from the weight of the soil contained inside. You can build a simple raised bed garden from 1x4 or 1x6 lumber set on edge and filled with a good grade of topsoil. A more attractive, deeper, and stronger raised-bed garden can be built from 2x6 or 2x8 lumber, two or more boards high. A top plate of 2x4 or 2x6 adds rigidity and strength to the unit and will also give you a seat all around the garden for tending the plants.

A basic construction rule that must be followed when building a raised-bed garden, no matter the design or material used, is that the bed must be staked in place to prevent bulging. Stakes should be at least twice as long as the walls of the bed are high and be buried so that their tops are flush with the top of the bed. Additionally, stakes should be placed in all corners and, spaced about two feet apart on all sides. Stakes can be set inside or outside, but the raised-bed will be more attractive if the stakes are placed in the interior, as in the illustration.

Materials List
▼▼▼▼▼▼▼▼▼▼▼▼▼▼▼▼▼▼▼▼▼▼▼

4' x 6' raised bed garden
All materials are 2x4 redwood or pressure-treated lumber

1. Front and back: 6' redwood (three required for each)
2. Sides: 4' redwood (three required per side)
3. Stakes: 24" long (ten required)
4. Top rail: 6' 4" redwood, mitered at ends (two required)
5. Top rail: 4' 4" redwood, mitered at ends (two required)
   Galvanized 16d nails, five pounds

▼▼▼

Build the basic frame in the desired garden location. Nail the long pieces into the ends of the short pieces using 16d galvanized nails. Once the frame has been built, use a post hole digger to dig holes for the support stakes. Spacing is all four corners and about two feet apart along the sides. Set the stakes and fill around them with soil and compact. Nail the frame to the stakes. Next, attach the top rails flat on top of frame. The top rail will cover the edges of the frame and the support stakes. When installed, the top rail is also a seat all around the raised-bed. Miter the ends of the top rails for a decorative, finished look. Countersink all nail holes. Fill the garden with a good grade topsoil, compost, and peatmoss. A wheelbarrow will be of use here. The raised bed is ready for planting.

ORCHARD LADDER

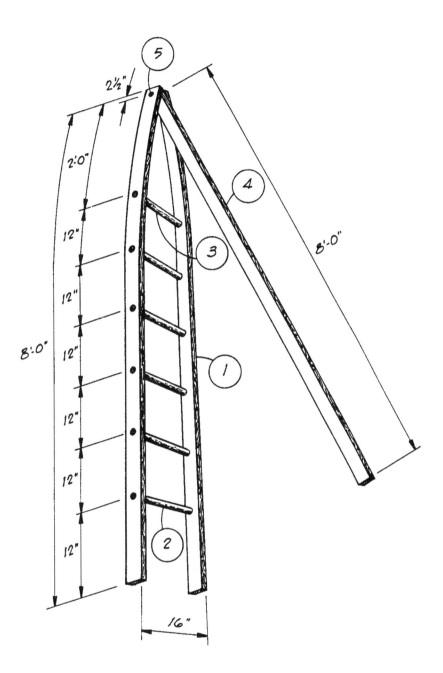

If you have fruit trees in your yard or garden, you know how difficult it can be to harvest the fruit. Folding ladders are generally not high (or safe) enough, extension ladders tend to break limbs, and climbing the tree to reach fruit is downright dangerous. Commercial orchards have an easy solution for picking fruit, a tripod-like orchard ladder. With this plan you can build one.

Materials List

▼▼▼▼▼▼▼▼▼▼▼▼▼▼▼▼▼▼▼▼▼▼

1. Side: 2" x 4" x 8' redwood (two required)
2. Rungs: 1" diameter, 16" (five required)
3. Top rung: 1" diameter, 15"
4. Support Leg: 2" x 4" x 8'
5. Top bolt (carriage bolt, 5½"), three washers and wing nut
   Waterproof adhesive
   6d galvanized finishing nails, one pound
   Exterior primer and paint, if desired.

▼▼▼

Mark the location of the rung holes on two of the 2x4s. Note in the diagram that these holes are spaced 12" apart, starting from the bottom, and are centered. Drill 1" holes at these locations.

Beginning with the bottom rung, apply a coat of adhesive to the end of a 16" long dowel and slip it into the first hole. When the end of the dowel is flush with the outside face of the side, drive a finishing nail through the edge of the 2x4 to hold the rung in place. You might have to drill to prevent splitting the rung. Continue installing the rungs on one side until you come to the last hole where the 15" rung is installed in the same manner. Now, repeat this process, installing the rungs on the other side of the ladder.

After all of the rungs are in place, you will have something that really resembles a ladder. Next, drill a bolt hole (2½" down from the top) on both sides of the ladder and on the support leg. These holes, which are for the top pivot bolt, should be centered on the sides and support leg. Start the bolt through one side of the ladder, pass through a washer, through the support leg, add another washer and pass through the second ladder leg. Add one more washer and the wing nut. Tighten the nut. Some force may be required here to bend the two ladder sides into position.

Once the top bolt is in position and the wing nut tightened, the ladder is ready to be used. The orchard ladder can be left in a natural state or primed and painted. Store out of the weather when not in use.

GARDEN BENCH

Garden bench - Courtesy, California Redwood Association

This redwood garden bench, courtesy of the California Redwood Association, is a handsome addition to any redwood deck or garden area. This bench is nail laminated and can be made in any reasonable length—4, 6, 8, 10 and 12 feet long. Use the more economical garden grades of redwood (construction common and merchantable redwood) for the seat, and construction heart redwood for the legs where increased decay resistance may be required.

To keep the seats even and level, build this bench on edge or upside down on a flat surface. For top performance use noncorrosive nails such as stainless steel, aluminum, or top quality, hot-dipped galvanized. To prevent splitting, drill nail holes near board ends.

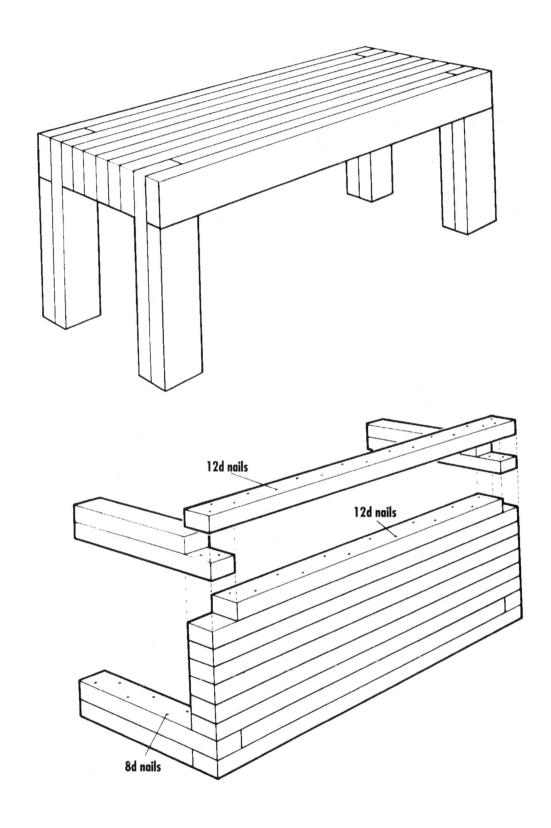

12d nails

12d nails

8d nails

Garden bench detail - Courtesy, California Redwood Association

Materials List
▼▼▼▼▼▼▼▼▼▼▼▼▼▼▼▼▼▼▼▼▼▼▼▼

For benches of five different lengths

Bench Length	Lumber, all 2x4s
4 feet	Two pieces 6' long Five pieces 8' long
6 feet	Twelve pieces 6' long
8 feet	Ten pieces 8' long Two pieces 6' long
10 feet	Ten pieces 10' long Two pieces 6' long
12 feet	Ten pieces 12' long Two pieces 6' long

▼▼

These benches are made entirely of 2x4 inch lumber. There are two basic elements, the legs and the seat.

Legs are built up with two 2x4s, one long piece and one short piece. Cut four pieces 18" long. Trim four short pieces about 14½" (Subtract the *actual* width of your 2x4 from 18" for this measurement.) To make legs, assemble short and long pieces in pairs with six 8-penny nails.

Seatboards are made by nail-laminating ten 2x4s together, creating the butcher-block appearance. The length of the 2x4s used for the seat will vary according to the length of the bench (see materials list). Trim two short pieces to accommodate the legs. Make sure the 2x4s are level and even on the top seating area. Use 12-penny nails every 6" in a zig-zag pattern. The seat may be planed after construction to level the seating area. To finish, allow the bench to weather naturally or coat with boiled linseed oil.

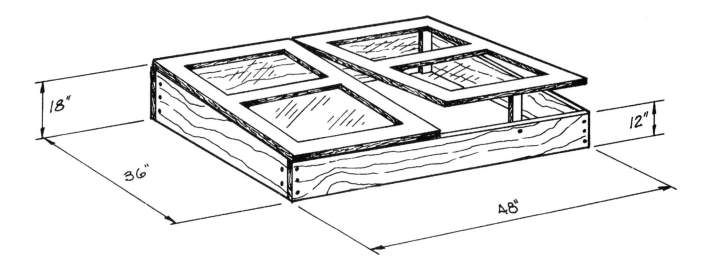

A well-built cold frame will allow you to start plants for your garden months before the growing season. For this reason, it is often called a "poor man's greenhouse." A cold frame can be as simple as a piece of glass covering a wooden box or as complex as a battery of internally heated and insulted growing chambers. The project in this section is a good, all-around cold frame that should provide years of useful service for the serious gardener.

A cold frame can be either free-standing or built against a south facing wall of an existing building. Overall dimensions are not etched in stone but some general guidelines should be followed. For example, the back wall of a cold frame should be about one and one half times as high as the front wall so that snow and rain water will run off naturally. While the size of a cold frame can vary, depending on the type of glazing used, a suitable size for most gardens is illustrated in this section.

Two types of materials can be used: dimensional lumber (2x4, 2x6, and 2x8) or exterior grade plywood. Both materials are suitable, but CDX plywood is easier to work with. One sheet of ¾" plywood is more than enough for this project.

Glazing for a cold frame can be expensive, but you can use old storm windows to cut costs. A standard size is 2' x 3' feet. You should have little problem locating second-hand windows. Garage sales are a good source.

Materials List
▼▼▼▼▼▼▼▼▼▼▼▼▼▼▼▼▼▼▼▼▼▼▼▼

All parts cut from ¾" CDX plywood

Front: 12" x 48"
Back: 18" x 48"
Sides: 34" long, 18" high at rear, 12" high at front (two required)
Top: wooden frame storm windows 2' x 3' (two required)
Internal bracing: 2x2 lumber - two 12" , two 18"
Hinges: two per window
Handle: one per window

▼▼▼

Cut the plywood as indicated in the materials list. Nail the face and back of
the unit to the sides. Then attach the internal bracing inside each corner.
Use waterproof adhesive and screws. Add the windows, mounting hinges
along the top. Position the wooden storm windows so that their frames
overlap the frame all around. Attach a handle to the top front of each
window. Now the cold frame is ready for service. Position this unit so that
the 12" front is on the south side, to get maximum sunlight and solar energy.
On cold days, keep the unit closed. On warm days, prop the windows open
with a stick, but be sure to close them at night.

Of all the owls, only two will make use of a bird house or nesting box. The saw-whet owl of the northern border area of the United States is one type, but it is rarely encountered. When found, however, it is extremely tame.

The more common screech owl is widely dispersed across the country and will take up residence in a nesting box. Both types of owls prefer a nesting box that is mounted on a tree or post from 10' to 12' above the ground.

Materials List
▼▼▼▼▼▼▼▼▼▼▼▼▼▼▼▼▼▼▼▼▼▼▼▼

All pieces cut from pine or redwood

Front: 1" x 7" x 16"
Back: 1" x 7" x 22"
Bottom: 1" x 7" x 7"
Top: 1" x 8½" x 11"
Sides: 1" x 8½" x 34" cut as indicated into two pieces
Waterproof woodworker's glue
6d finishing nails
Exterior primer and paint is desired
One 3" long screw hook
One 2" long woodscrew

▼▼

Owl nesting box piece cutting diagram

Cut all pieces based on the materials list and cutting diagram. Cut a 3" diameter hole in the face of the front piece, with the center located 5" down from the top edge. Drill four ¾" holes for drainage in the bottom piece. Drill a ½" hole in the back panel for mounting. Locate this mounting hole 3" down from the top and centered.

Assemble the pieces by first attaching the side panels to the back piece. Next, add the bottom piece, front, and finally the top. Use adhesive and finishing nails.

Now the nesting box can be primed and painted or allowed to weather naturally. Mount the box on a pole or tree by putting a screw hook at the proper height and hanging the box by hooking the box over the hole in the back of the box. Additional stability can be achieved by driving a 2" screw below the box, through the back panel and into the tree or post.

CHAPTER 5
MISCELLANEOUS PROJECTS
▼▼▼▼▼▼▼▼▼▼▼▼▼▼▼▼▼▼▼▼▼▼▼▼▼▼▼▼▼▼▼▼▼▼▼▼

BICYCLE RACK

A storage rack for bicycles will greatly help to organize your garage or yard because it provides a place for bicycles when they are not in use. While a bike rack takes up some space, it is much easier to use for women and small children than screw hooks for hanging bicycles.

Materials List

▼▼▼▼▼▼▼▼▼▼▼▼▼▼▼▼▼▼▼▼▼▼▼

One sheet: ½" CDX plywood
Two: 2" x 2" x 48"
Two: 2" x 2" x 33"
Waterproof adhesive
Thirty: 1" long wood screws
Exterior primer and paint

▼▼

Cut two 3' x 4' panels from the plywood. Mark the location of the cutouts on one panel. Each is 3" wide, 3" up from the bottom and 6" down from the top. Position them 4½" in from each side and 6" apart. Make the cuts using the plunge cut with a saber saw. Make another panel exactly the same.

Sandwich the 2" x 2" x 48" lumber between the top and bottom edges and, the 2" x 2" x 33" lumber along the sides, using adhesive and screws. Position the 2x2s even with the edges of the panel before fastening.

Next, cut the remaining plywood panel (2' x 4') into two 2' squares. Cut each of these so that the top comes to a point. Attach these side panels to the sides of the bike rack, keeping the bottom edges parallel. Use adhesive and screws.

Sand all surfaces and paint with exterior primer. Apply two coats of exterior paint, allowing sufficient drying time between coats. Now the bike rack is ready to be placed into service.

WHIRLIGIG

Whirligigs are fun woodworking projects that can be made from scrap lumber. They make wonderful gifts as most people like the way they twirl with the slightest breeze. A table saw, with a ripping fence, makes it easy to cut the strips of lumber into the right thickness.

Materials List
▼▼▼▼▼▼▼▼▼▼▼▼▼▼▼▼▼▼▼▼▼▼▼▼

Thirty-five strips of scrap lumber: ½" x ¾" x 8"
One threaded steel rod: ¼" diameter, 12" long
Three nuts, two washers
Nylon cord, dark color, 24" long
Fishing swivel, size 2 or 3

▼▼

Rip the scrap lumber with the grain to the size listed. Drill a ¼" hole in each piece, centered on the flat side. While a hand-held electric drill can be used for this, a drill press set up to drill each piece will make the work go much quicker.

Drill a ¹⁄₁₆" hole across one end of the steel rod. Use a high carbon drill bit. It is through this hole that the fishing swivel will later be installed.

Pass the threaded rod through all of the strips. Next, add one washer and a nut to the end of the rod which has a hole. Place a washer and two nuts on the other end of the rod. Tighten the double nuts, with two wrenches, to lock them together. Using a wrench on each end of the whirligig, tighten until the piece is nearly rigid.

Pass the open end of the fishing swivel through the hole in the threaded rod and clamp closed. Next tie one end of the nylon cord to the top of the fishing swivel. The cord is used for hanging the whirligig.

Move the strips so that each end passes to the right of the stick above. The effect is a spiral of strips. After all strips have been so turned, tighten the nuts further, locking the whirligig in a spiral shape.

The whirligig can be finished with linseed oil or left in a natural state. If finishing is desired, paint with linseed oil, start at the top and work down. Now the whirligig is ready for hanging outdoors or for gift giving.

WOODEN BASE FOR SHARPENING STONE

Many sharpening stones are available to the outdoorsman for keeping knives sharp. While putting a keen edge on a knife is not difficult, it requires that the knife blade be held at a 15° angle as it is passed over the surface of a sharpening stone. While most directions for sharpening call for the stone to be placed on a workbench during sharpening, the common practice is to hold the stone in the palm of one hand as the knife is held with the other hand. Because most sharpening stones are rather thin, usually less than ¾", the risk of nicking one's fingers during the sharpening process is great.

One good solution to this problem is to make a wooden base for your sharpening stone that will allow you to hold a sharpening stone without any risk of cutting yourself. A wooden base can be made from a scrap piece of lumber, but a much more attractive and functional base can be made from a piece of hardwood.

You do not have to have a stone of the size listed below to make this base. If your stone is not this size, measure it, then work with a block of wood that is 2" longer than the stone, and 1" wider and thicker. Set your router so when you have routed the position for the stone, the stone will be ¼" higher than the block.

Materials List
▾▾▾▾▾▾▾▾▾▾▾▾▾▾▾▾▾▾▾▾▾▾▾▾▾▾

One sharpening stone: 4¼" x 1⅝" x ½"
Hardwood block: 2½" x 6¼" x 1½"

▾▾

Cut the hardwood block to the size indicated in the materials list. Then trace the outline of the sharpening stone onto the top of the block. The sharpening stone should be centered on the block before tracing its outline. Next, using a ½" straight router bit, remove material inside the tracing. The depth setting on the router for this operation should be ¼". Since this operation must be done freehand, make certain that the hardwood block is securely fastened—a woodworker's vise is ideal for this.

Next, using a hand-held router fitted with a Roman ogee bit, put a decorative edge around the top of the hardwood block. If this rather specialized router bit is not available, you can sand the top edges of the block for a finished edge.

After routing, check the fit of the sharpening stone in the center of the wooden block. If necessary, remove more wood with a wood chisel. Once you are satisfied with the fit of the stone—it should be reasonably snug—apply a coat of linseed oil to the block and your sharpening stone base is ready for service.

BOOT SCRAPER

Modern hiking boots are great for walking on difficult terrain as the patterned soles grab the surface and enable us to walk or climb without slipping. Unfortunately, these same soles are also great for picking up soil, mud, and snow. In the field, this presents little problem, but when we walk in the house, these materials come with us and are often deposited on carpeting and vinyl floors. I got tired of tracking dirt and mud into the house, even with flat soled shoes, and developed this handy boot scraper.

Our boot scraper is just outside the back door where it is used by all family members before entering. The stiff bristle brushes will quickly remove dirt, mud, snow, and any other material on the soles of any type of footwear. The secret to effective use is to place one foot on each side of the scraper. Then, while transferring all body weight to one foot, lift the other to the brushes and clean off the soles of that boot or shoe. Then switch and clean the other foot.

Material List

▾▾▾▾▾▾▾▾▾▾▾▾▾▾▾▾▾▾▾▾▾▾▾▾

Four scrub brushes (natural bristles), 7¼" x 2¼"
One piece ¾" CDX plywood, 10" x 29"
Four pieces lumber, 1" x 4" x 10"
Four 2" x 2" metal angle brackets with mounting
   screws
Waterproof adhesive
Eight ¼" woodscrews

▾▾▾

Cut all pieces as indicated in the materials list. Next, glue and screw two of the brushes to the center of the ¾" plywood. Keep the long edges tight together, pointing across the plywood, as shown in the photo. Attach with adhesive and screws two pieces of 1x4 lumber one on each side of the brushes. Next, attach the two remaining scrub brushes on top of the 1x4s. Install each brush on edge, bristles facing towards the center and over the base brushes. Use two angle brackets to hold each brush in place. The brushes must be far enough apart so that a boot will fit between them.

WALKING STICK ————————————————

A walking stick is handy when taking a casual stroll along trails or paths in the city or country. When backpacking, a walking stick rather quickly will change you from a biped into a triped and thus greatly reduce your chances of falling when walking over difficult terrain or fording a stream. While commercially made walking sticks are available in backpacking shops across the country, the handy woodworker can make one quite easily in the shop from a variety of materials.

▼▼

Some of the more common materials include bamboo, discarded garden tool handles, PVC pipe, and seasoned hardwood.

Bamboo makes an ideal walking stick when the proper diameter (approximately 1") is cut to a suitable length for your height. A six-foot hiker should find a 42" length just right. Since bamboo is as strong as brass, you can really count on a walking stick made from this material to not only hold your weight but to flex somewhat during use. Another advantage of bamboo is, of course, its lightness. Wrap the top 8" with leather for a comfortable grip.

Discarded garden tool handles also make suitable walking sticks. Cut one to the proper length and sand any rough areas. The top end of the shaft should be rounded to reduce the chances of hand blisters and the bottom should be slightly pointed. You can apply a saturating coat of linseed oil to prevent cracking or checking.

PVC pipe will make a dual purpose walking stick that should appeal to the wilderness fishermen as it can also be a fishing rod case. To make one of these, measure your favorite two-piece fishing rod. Next, purchase a piece of 1¼" diameter PVC pipe long enough to hold the rod sections. Buy two end caps and some adhesive as well. Glue one of the caps on one end of the pipe. Place your rodless reel into the pipe and put the second cap on the other end of the pipe. Obviously, the top cap is not attached with adhesive. Put a piece of tape just below the removable cap so you can tell at a glance which end is the top. Now the next time you hike into your favorite wilderness lake, not only will you have a walking stick to help you get there, but when you do, you can be certain that your fishing rod makes the trip in good shape as well.

Seasoned hardwood maple, ash, hickory, or other hardwoods can also be used to make a walking stick. Whittle the bottom end of the shaft into a point and rounding off the top end. You can wrap the bottom with soft wire to prevent splitting and wrap the top with leather to provide a soft grip.

FIELD BOX FOR PHOTOGRAPHIC ——— & OPTICAL EQUIPMENT

Photographic and optical equipment can take a real beating in the field, especially if kept in traditional soft cases. While hard cases are available for cameras and accessories, they are expensive and, more often than not, are not suitable for specific field needs. A good solution is to build a custom-sized, waterproof field box in the home workshop.

The directions given in this section result in a plywood field box which measures 13½" x 10¾" and 10" high. I have found this size to be more than adequate for safely holding one Nikon camera body, four lenses, film, filters, spotting scope, and binoculars while in the field.

Materials List

▼▼▼▼▼▼▼▼▼▼▼▼▼▼▼▼▼▼▼▼▼▼

Top and bottom, 12¾" x 10" x ¾" CDX plywood (two required)
Front and back, 10" x 13½" x ⅜" CDX plywood (two required)
Sides, 10" x 10" x ⅜" CDX plywood (two required)
Two hinges
Hasp
Carrying handle
Closed cell foam such as Ensolite
Waterproof adhesive
6d finishing nails
Caulking

▼▼▼

Cut the pieces based on the materials list. Using adhesive and finishing nails, attach the front, back, and sides to the bottom. Next, install the top. Mark the front, sides, and back of the box with a line placed 3" down from the top. Cut the box along this line.

Attach the top section to the bottom section using hinges installed on the back. Attach the hasp to the front of the box. Caulk all interior seams. Attach the handle to the top. Prime and paint the box if desired, or apply a clear finish.

Make the interior of your field box customized for the photographic and optical equipment you plan to carry. Do this by cutting the closed cell foam to cover all interior surfaces. You must also cut pieces of foam for individual pieces of equipment as required. Or you can carry your lenses and other equipment in their soft cases as I do.